T0302830

Sustainment of Army Forces in Operation Iraqi Freedom

Major Findings and Recommendations

Eric Peltz, Marc L. Robbins, Kenneth J. Girardini,
Rick Eden, John M. Halliday, Jeffrey Angers

Prepared for the United States Army

Approved for public release; distribution unlimited

ARROYO CENTER

The research described in this report was sponsored by the United States Army under Contract No. DASW01-01-C-0003.

Library of Congress Cataloging-in-Publication Data

Sustainment of army forces in operation Iraqi freedom / Eric Peltz ... [et al.].
    p. cm.
    "MG-342."
    Includes bibliographical references.
    ISBN 0-8330-3783-8 (pbk.)
    1. Iraq War, 2003—Equipment and supplies. 2. Iraq War, 2003—Logistics.
   3. Military supplies. I. Peltz, Eric, 1968–

DS79.76.S873 2005
956.7044'38—dc22

                              2005007010

The RAND Corporation is a nonprofit research organization providing objective analysis and effective solutions that address the challenges facing the public and private sectors around the world. RAND's publications do not necessarily reflect the opinions of its research clients and sponsors.

RAND® is a registered trademark.

Department of Defense photo by Master Sergeant Mark Bucher, U.S. Air Force.

Published 2005 by the RAND Corporation
1776 Main Street, P.O. Box 2138, Santa Monica, CA 90407-2138
1200 South Hayes Street, Arlington, VA 22202-5050
201 North Craig Street, Suite 202, Pittsburgh, PA 15213-1516
RAND URL: http://www.rand.org/
To order RAND documents or to obtain additional information, contact
Distribution Services: Telephone: (310) 451-7002;
Fax: (310) 451-6915; Email: order@rand.org

Preface

This monograph describes how well the Department of Defense logistics system met the materiel sustainment needs of Army forces in Operation Iraqi Freedom, documents the major reasons for shortfalls in performance, provides recommendations for improvement, and points to questions raised with respect to the design of future forces. The findings should be of interest throughout the Army as well the broader Department of Defense supply chain and force development communities.

The monograph summarizes the results of a research project called "Army Logistics in OIF: Key Issues for the Army," sponsored by the Deputy Chief of Staff, G-4, Headquarters, Department of the Army. The purpose of the project was to identify key issues for near-term improvement and future force logistics system development. A series of companion monographs will address many of the topics in this volume in more detail and should be useful for those seeking an in-depth examination of performance, rigorous analysis of the causes of shortfalls, and ideas for improvement. They will include analyses of:

- Battlefield logistics and effects on operations.
- Spare parts demand analysis and deployed authorized stockage lists (ASLs).
- Army Prepositioned Stock (APS) ASLs.
- APS war reserve secondary item inventory stored in the United States and forward positioned.
- Methods and processes for determining and resourcing national-level spare part requirements.
- End-to-end distribution.

This research has been conducted in RAND Arroyo Center's Military Logistics Program. RAND Arroyo Center, part of the RAND Corporation, is a federally funded research and development center sponsored by the United States Army.

Questions and comments regarding this research are welcome and should be directed to the leaders of the research team, Eric Peltz and Marc Robbins, at peltz@rand.org and robbins@rand.org.

For more information on RAND Arroyo Center, contact the Director of Operations (telephone 310-393-0411, extension 6419; FAX 310-451-6952; email Marcy_Agmon@rand.org), or visit Arroyo's web site at http://www.rand.org/ard/.

Contents

Figures

Tables

Summary

Although Army units always had sufficient sustainment support to accomplish their missions and execute operations as planned, during Operation Iraqi Freedom's major combat operations through the fall of Baghdad, on-hand supplies held by maneuver forces were lower than planned for all commodities except fuel. This was driven by limited theater transportation capacity. The supply of subsistence items, such as food and water, gradually improved, but spare parts support continued to be plagued by distribution problems well into stability and support operations (SASO). Moreover, for spare parts, distribution problems were compounded by national supply shortages as operations continued at a high pace into the fall of 2003 and beyond.

When the ground forces attacked on 21 March 2003, there simply were not enough cargo trucks to meet all of the demands. A confluence of factors created the situation:

- Mobilization and deployment planning produced fewer trucks than requested.
- A change in the troop support plan—to supply bottled water throughout operations rather than rely solely on "bulk" water—more than doubled the cargo truck requirement.
- *Fedayeen* attacks prevented the early, anticipated use of commercial trucking to supplement the Army's capacity.
- Trucks were used to move units to secure supply lines, an unexpected requirement.
- Road conditions were worse than reconnaissance indicated, slowing movement.
- Extremely bad weather brought convoys to a halt.

Despite this "perfect storm" of factors, units carried enough supplies across the border to weather the situation until a fairly steady flow of critical supplies could be established, although it was insufficient to establish unit or intermediate supply buffers. However, a lack of effective automation to provide situational awareness greatly limited visibility of the flow of supplies moving toward units. The resulting uncertainty increased the perceived level of supply risk on the battlefield. A related lack of mobile, non-line-of-sight (NLOS) communications equipment prevented units from being able to use their automated systems to order parts during combat operations, further disrupting the spare parts supply chain. Unit-level spare parts inventories were not designed to have the quantities of items needed to handle the supply chain disruptions and delays, and the spares inventories in prepositioned unit sets drawn by the 3rd Infantry Division had an ineffective mix of parts, in contrast to the parts they left at home, stemming from problems with the requirements determination process for prepositioned stock.

Many distribution problems for spare parts originated in how Defense Logistics Agency (DLA)-managed distribution centers and Air Mobility Command aerial ports in the continental United States (CONUS) packaged shipments for delivery to the theater. These problems started during the force buildup in Kuwait in January and extended well into SASO. An ineffective process for communicating address codes for deployed Army units and then entering those codes into the DLA information system prevented the usual practice of consolidating small items for each brigade (and other similar-sized units) into large brigade-level boxes. Instead, many boxes initially contained items for a mix of addresses in theater, leading to delays and mis-shipments. Then a lack of a DLA understanding of Army distribution structures at the theater, division, and support battalion levels led to a misalignment between how shipments were consolidated on pallets in CONUS for air transport and theater distribution capabilities, leading to further delays in theater, as pallets for air cargo were generally mixed across brigades. As the SASO operating tempo exceeded expectations, another problem emerged to contribute to distribution delays: demand for spare parts outstripped the capacity of the distribution centers. It took about three-quarters of a year to gain approval for and build sufficient capacity to handle the volume and to work off the backlogs.

As SASO continued at a heavy pace into the summer of 2003 and beyond, national stock availability became an increasing problem, pushing backorders for Army-managed spare parts as high as 35 percent. War reserve requirements missed many critical items and were poorly resourced, making them of relatively little value in meeting the Army's requirement for spare parts until a production surge could "kick in." Additionally, planning guidance limited war reserve stocks to five months of combat operations, which is shorter than the lead times for many parts. Despite limited spare part war reserves, a production surge was not initiated until the second half of 2003, several months into OIF, as the result of slow requirements and funding approval. Further, the initial production surge that was eventually funded ended up being insufficient, stemming from forecasting problems and the mismatch between the actual and anticipated SASO operating pace. With long production lead times for many items, full recovery from these problems is extending into 2005. Finally, the limited national supply levels and issues with forward positioned war reserve and theater supply base planning led to what have been considered excessive air shipping costs. Much less costly transport by ship is infeasible except when inventories are available to fill the slower surface pipeline.

We conclude that the problems with the materiel sustainment of Army units that have been exposed in OIF stem from several, cross-cutting issues:

- The lack of a joint, DoD-wide vision of how the supply chain should operate that lays out guiding principles for each node, channel, and organization.
- Within-organization policies that are not aligned with a common vision and each other as well as process design and execution problems.
- A lack of training exercises for theater startup and logistics crisis action planning, which contributes to process execution problems and makes it difficult to expose design problems.
- Deliberate planning guidance focused solely on major combat operations, contributing to underfunding of critical reserve capacity.
- Crisis action planning and resourcing that failed to protect against moderate uncertainty.
- Limited investment in logistics automation, in-transit visibility, and communication systems.
- A lack of theater distribution planning and decision-support tools.
- Organizational structures not well designed to support expeditionary deployment planning and operations.

This report examines the root causes of supply chain problems to the extent possible and offers recommendations designed to address these issues. Some of the recommendations set a "foundation" for the others based upon a linked high-level supply chain architecture:

- The newly designated Distribution Process Owner (USTRANSCOM), in concert with the Army, its sister services, and DLA, should develop and promulgate a supply chain vision articulating the complementary roles of production, inventory, and distribution, which includes transportation, movement control, transshipment operations, and shipment preparation. The first chapter of this report offers a recommended vision, with the remainder of the report focused on gaps between OIF sustainment and this vision.
- Every joint logistics organization should examine and refine its processes to ensure detailed alignment with the supply chain vision.
- Metrics, in conjunction with automated signaling systems for process monitoring and control, should be adopted to facilitate command and control efforts to maintain alignment with the vision, especially as contingencies place demand and supply "shocks" on the logistics system.

- All processes should be exercised on a periodic basis to check alignment with the vision and ensure that personnel are well-trained, especially for processes only executed during contingencies.

General recommendations that build upon this foundation include:

- Information system resourcing for logistics units needs higher priority. Non-line-of-sight, mobile communications and logistics and operational situational awareness capabilities are essential for logistics forces supporting distributed operations over extended distances.

- While differing in the nature of demands, SASO can be as or even more logistically demanding than major combat operations and need equal attention in joint sustainment planning. Deliberate planning guidance should be reviewed to assess whether the scenarios provide an adequate basis for resource planning. Within the Army, this would affect the force structure process and war reserve planning. For DLA and USTRANSCOM, this may affect the design of strategic distribution capacity. Planning for contingency operations should also include consideration of SASO requirements—what does it take to "win the peace"?

- Resourcing processes should consider uncertainty and more appropriately weigh the implications of capacity shortages, as even relatively small, quickly resolved shortfalls can have extended effects arising from the buildup of backlogs. Surprises and forecasting errors must be expected. Thus, supply and force risk assessments during planning should recognize the relatively long-term operational effects of insufficient capacity that arise from the difficulty of working off a backlog while simultaneously handling a higher level of demand, affecting decisions about how much slack or buffer capacity should be in the system. Additionally, resourcing processes must be responsive, with decisionmakers made fully cognizant of the implications of delay, and the supply chain from the industrial base to tactical distribution capability must be agile enough to respond.

- Joint and interagency training should be extended to exercise the entire logistics system as it will have to operate in wartime, from contingency planning and resourcing through redeployment. The Army and its supply chain partners should review all wartime and contingency processes from the tactical to the national level to determine which ones are not fully exercised in training, with all requisite organizations participating. The same review should determine which tasks do not have adequate doctrine and mission training plans upon which to base training.

- Planning tools and organizational structures need to better support expeditionary operations. First, to support fast-paced, frequently changing expeditionary operations, logistics system planners need effective automation to rapidly determine capability requirements as operational requirements change. Second, organizational structures should be designed to enable these requirements to be easily and quickly resourced. Third, the structures and automation should support effective deployment planning.

Specifically, the report recommends that the Army:

- Redesign the methodology for developing prepositioned unit-level spare parts inventories (authorized stockage lists) to ensure that units will have an effective mix of parts to maintain readiness.
- Configure prepositioned ASL storage to support expeditionary operations. This will enable rapid deployment with immediate, sustainable employment.
- Improve the ability to change ASLs when task organization changes, which hampered support in some situations during major combat operations.
- Increase tactical inventory per item quantities to accommodate contingency demand rates and to cover a reasonable range of contingency distribution conditions, to include short disruptions and longer delivery times than experienced in garrison.
- Provide mobile, NLOS communications capability to all key logistics nodes.
- Develop and field effective and adequately distributed logistics and operational situational awareness capabilities for logistics units.
- Develop improved theater distribution planning automation.
- Practice joint theater setup planning.
- Plan for bottled water (until alternative solutions are developed that satisfy field needs) and plan for sufficient cargo trucks to meet this requirement.
- Create modular logistics organizational designs that more effectively support phased theater opening to support expeditionary operations.
- Create distribution center units to improve theater distribution setup capabilities.
- Focus forward positioned war reserve sustainment stocks on big, heavy items, and stock theater and national inventories with sufficient quantities of these items to support replenishment by sealift.
- Redesign the war reserve determination process (forward positioned and CONUS).
- Align war reserve funding with its intended role in contingency operations.
- Include SASO requirements in the war reserve determination process.
- Improve the speed and accuracy of the national-level spare parts contingency forecasting process.

- Redesign the spare parts contingency funding process to make it responsive to contingency support requirements.
- Practice (exercise) the contingency forecasting and funding processes.
- Work with DLA and USTRANSCOM and its subordinate commands to:
  - Improve unit addressing information flow and system usage.
  - Align joint load policy with Army unit capabilities.
  - Reexamine roles of aerial ports in load building to assess what materiel they should consolidate for shipment versus DLA distribution centers.
  - Increase CONUS distribution center wartime capacity expansion speed and evaluate capacity planning adequacy.
- Introduce standard consideration of uncertainty and risk management in planning processes with capabilities embedded in automated decision-support tools.

The adoption of these recommendations will better prepare the U.S. Army and the DoD more broadly to conduct future contingency operations. Some would help improve support to ongoing operations in Iraq, and many are being acted upon by the U.S. Army or are consistent with Army initiatives.

Acknowledgments

This research was commissioned by and guided by LTG Claude V. Christianson (Deputy Chief of Staff, G-4, Headquarters, Department of the Army), MG Terry Juskowiak (Commanding General of the Combined Arms Support Command), and MG Mitchell Stevenson (Deputy Chief of Staff, G-3, Army Materiel Command). They asked us to take an objective look at logistics performance in Operation Iraqi Freedom to help establish the hard facts on which to build a firm foundation for the development of improved logistics capabilities and to develop specific recommendations for the Army to consider, reflecting one of the hallmarks of the U.S. Army: taking hard, critical looks at everything it does to continuously improve capabilities. In this spirit, the Army's logistics leadership has been deeply engaged in this research as we have presented emerging findings, immediately acting upon many "interim" findings and recommendations and incorporating others into longer-term improvement efforts.

Throughout the course of the research process, we appreciate the feedback and thought-provoking discussions generated during in-progress reviews by GEN Paul Kern, LTG Richard Hack, MG William Mortenson, MG Daniel Mongeon, MG N. Ross Thompson, MG James Pillsbury, MG Brian Geehan, MG Mike Lenaers, MG Charlie Fletcher, BG Kathy Gainey, Mr. Tom Edwards, Mr. Fred Baillie, Ms. Claudia Knott, Mr. William Neal, Ms. Modell Plummer, BG Steve Anderson, COL Jim Rentz, and COL Robert Carpenter.

We thank the myriad number of people who gave their time for interviews and provided data to us throughout the Army, the Defense Logistics Agency, and the U.S. Transportation Command.

At RAND, the programming and database support provided by Candice Riley, Pat Boren, and Tim Colvin have been essential to the success of this research. Art Lackey has frequently provided his technical expertise to help us delve into the causes of problems. Jim Quinlivan and LTG (ret.) Vince Russo provided high-quality reviews that helped us think about how to tell a complex story and raised many thought-provoking issues that pushed us to examine the adequacy of recommendations. Pamela Thompson has provided excellent support in preparing this report and several others in the series, and Nikki Shacklett provided a helpful edit.

Before completing his outstanding and dedicated service to the U.S. Army and RAND as the director of RAND Arroyo Center's Military Logistics Program in April 2004 after eight years, John Dumond's appreciation of the issues and critical eye helped us develop the research and fine tune the messages.

Glossary

ABN	Airborne Division
ACR	Armored Cavalry Regiment
AD	Armored Division
ADA	Air Defense Artillery
AHR	Attack Helicopter Regiment
AMC	Army Materiel Command
AMI	Army-Managed Items
APOD	Aerial Port of Debarkation
APOE	Aerial Port of Embarkation
APS	Army Prepositioned Stock
ARCENT	U.S. Army Central Command
ASL	Authorized Stockage List
AVN	Aviation
AWCF	Army Working Capital Fund
AWRS	Army War Reserve Sustainment
BCS3	Battle Command Sustainment Support System
BCT	Brigade Combat Team
BN	Battalion
C2	Command and Control
CASCOM	Combined Arms Support Command
CAV	Cavalry
CCP	Consolidation and Containerization Point

CDC	Corps Distribution Center
CENTCOM	U.S. Central Command
CFLCC	Coalition Forces Land Component Command
CIF	Candidate Items Files
CONOPS	Contingency Operations
CONUS	Continental United States
COSCOM	Corps Support Command
CR	Cavalry Regiment
CSB	Corps Support Battalion
CSG	Corps Support Group
DBL	Distribution Based Logistics
DDSP	Defense Distribution Depot Susquehanna, PA
DISCOM	Division Support Command
Distribution	The process of moving materiel from a source to final destination, which includes the use and management of transportation resources, packaging, transshipment, and cross-docking operations
DIVARTY	Division Artillery
DLA	Defense Logistics Agency
DoD	Department of Defense
DODAAC	Department of Defense Activity Address Code
DON	Document Order Number
DPICM	Dual Purpose Improved Conventional Munitions
DPO	Distribution Process Owner
DS	Direct Support
DSB	Division Support Battalion
DSS	Distribution Support System
DTRACS	Defense Transportation and Control System
EDA	Equipment Downtime Analyzer
FSB	Forward Support Battalion
GS	General Support

GSA	General Services Agency
HQDA	Headquarters, Department of the Army
HS	Home Station
ID	Infantry Division
ILAP	Integrated Logistics Analysis Program
IPDS	Inland Petroleum Distribution System
ISB	Intermediate Support Base
ITV	In-Transit Visibility
JDLM	Joint Deployment and Logistics Model
KCIA	Kuwait City International Airport
LOC	Line of Communication
LRP	Logistics Release Point
LSA	Logistics Support Area
MEB	Marine Expeditionary Brigade
MEF	Marine Expeditionary Force
MEU	Marine Expeditionary Unit
MILALOC	Military Air Line of Communication
Movement Control	The command and control of transportation assets to ensure that they are effectively used to meet distribution needs
MRE	Meals Ready to Eat
MRO	Materiel Release Order
MSB	Main Support Battalion
MSR	Main Supply Route
MTO&E	Modified Table of Organization and Equipment
MTS	Movement Tracking System
NLOS	Non-Line-of-Sight
OA	Obligation Authority
ODS	Operation Desert Storm
OIF	Operation Iraqi Freedom
OIF 1	Initial set of deployments for OIF

OIF 2	The second set of units to be deployed, comprising a major force rotation early in 2004
OSD	Office of the Secretary of Defense
PDA	Personal Digital Assistant
PLL	Prescribed Load List
POL	Petroleum, Oil, and Lubricants
PPBE	Planning, Programming, Budgeting, and Execution
RFID	Radio Frequency Identification
RO	Requisitions Objective
RON	Request Order Number
ROP	Reorder Point
RWT	Requisition Wait Time
SARSS	Standard Army Retail Supply System
SASO	Stability and Support Operations
SC	Support Center
SDDC	Surface Distribution and Deployment Command
SDP	Strategic Distribution Platform
SMA	Supply Management Army
SPOD	Sea Port of Debarkation
SPOE	Sea Port of Embarkation
SSA	Supply Support Activity
Supply	Function responsible for the acquisition, receipt, storage, issue, and management of materiel
Supply Chain	All of the functions, organizations, and processes that combine to provided needed materiel to consumers
Supply Chain Management	The process of orchestrating all of the functions, organizations, and processes that combine to provide needed materiel to consumers
Sustainment	The provision of personnel, supplies, equipment, and services required to maintain and prolong operations or combat until successful accomplishment or revision of the mission or of the national objective

TDC	Theater Distribution Center
TO&E	Table of Organization and Equipment
Transportation	The function and assets used to move materiel and personnel
TSC	Theater Support Command
UA	Unit of Action
USAREUR	U.S. Army Europe
USTC	U.S. Transportation Command
USTRANSCOM	U.S. Transportation Command
WRSI	War Reserve Secondary Item

CHAPTER ONE

Sustainment of Army Units in OIF

By virtually every account, the major combat operations of Operation Iraqi Freedom (OIF) that toppled Saddam Hussein's regime in the spring of 2003 were a remarkable success. Yet there is a general belief within the Army and the broader defense community, supported by our analysis, that this success was achieved despite logistics problems that hampered materiel sustainment. However, moving beyond the initial impressions that emerged quickly following operations, our research also has led us to conclude that forces and sustainment capabilities were sufficiently robust to overcome the problems and effectively execute missions. Moreover, while there were legitimate issues, the great success of combat operations in Iraq could not have been achieved without logistics support that not only got the job done, but also was historically noteworthy in terms of the support concepts employed, the fast pace of operations to be supported, and strategic constraints on deployment that dictated relatively lean support in terms of units and supplies.

The basic strategic plan itself was predicated on a bold operational plan with a long, rapid advance enabled by the application of a new paradigm of logistics support termed distribution based logistics (DBL)[1] and a "running start" in which operations would begin before the full deployment of both combat and support forces in order

---

[1] DBL means providing support through frequent, reliable distribution flows with focused and right-sized inventories well positioned across the supply chain to cover consumption between replenishment cycles at the point of use and to buffer against distribution disruptions (examples of what is called special cause variability) and typical variability (i.e., the amount of variability experienced when processes are in control and working to "standard" or what is called common cause variability). The sizes of the buffers should be based upon risk tolerance with regard to the types of disruptions that can be weathered, replenishment frequency, and process effectiveness. As processes improve (i.e., the standard changes), reducing variability and increasing responsiveness, buffers can be decreased. Inventories at different "levels" in the supply chain on the battlefield should not be viewed as echelons of supply but rather as well-positioned risk mitigation measures to cover typical demand and distribution variability and to ensure that there are no breaks in support even when there are short breaks in the flow. Thus this inventory does not have to cover all items, just those that are essential for a given period of time under plausible conditions. The goal of DBL is not inventory reduction, it is improved support effectiveness and agility. However, when well executed, the total theater inventory will generally be lower than what had been required in the past. One might think of it as the appropriate amount to adequately mitigate risk without creating significant waste and overburdening mobility requirements. This contrasts with the notion of never having too much, which does not recognize the costs of inventory in terms of responding to shifting conditions, whether with regard to location or the nature of an operation, and in terms of the workload and process effectiveness burdens it imposes.

to achieve tactical and operational surprise.[2] To achieve continuous pressure and maintain the desired rapidity of advance until reaching and cordoning Baghdad—taking it quickly was not an assumed part of the plan—the force would not have the luxury of stopping to build up large supply points between Kuwait and Baghdad during the initial phase of combat, thus demanding the reliance on DBL. Operational commanders recognize that this plan led to some logistics risk that arose from initial limited sustainment capacity, especially with respect to critical transportation assets to deliver supplies as the competing demands of the "running start" and achieving robust support collided. However, they suggest that accepting the associated logistics stress was worth it, because surprise was achieved, contributing to the quick initial advance and rapid regime collapse.[3] It should also be noted that even though significant supply line interdiction was not deemed likely, especially once Iraqi army and Republican Guard units were defeated, another risk inherent in the plan was unsecured supply lines. This risk was accepted to enable a long, fast, continuous advance that kept the preponderance of striking power at the tip of the spear with the limited forces that the "running start" would initially provide. However, unanticipated resistance from Iraqi irregulars or *Fedayeen* dictated a change in this portion of the plan, which contributed to an interim pause of close to a week, as there was a wait for units to secure urban areas in the rear that were astride supply lines. But even with this pause, operational commanders suggest that the advance, combined with the surprise achieved by the "running start," was still fast enough to achieve their intent and probably minimized the length of major combat operations depicted in Figure 1.1. Additionally, executing DBL concepts revealed—and in some cases reinforced—doctrinal, organizational, training, equipment, and other resource issues that need to be addressed, but the logistics system did not break in the face of a logistically demanding operation.

The purpose of our research that produced this report has been to critically analyze materiel sustainment performance during major combat operations and stability and support operations, identify key issues that affected the performance, and recommend ways to improve future sustainment capabilities and the logistics system's robustness. The research should help move the Army and DoD from primarily anecdotally based first impressions from OIF to more objective measures of sustain-

---

[2] LtGen James Conway, commander, First Marine Expeditionary Force, "Live Briefing from Iraq," 30 May 2003, http://www.defenselink.mil/transcripts/2003/tr20030530-0229.html. LTG David D. McKiernan, "Operation Iraqi Freedom Briefing," 23 April 2003, www.defenselink.mil/transcripts/2003/tr20030423-0122.html.

[3] Conway; McKiernan. COL (ret.) Gregory Fontenot, LTC E. J. Degen, and LTC David Tohn conclude that the "tensions" from the running and early start "are a defining characteristic of the entire operation" (in *On Point: The United States Army in Operation Iraqi Freedom*, Fort Leavenworth, KS: Combat Studies Institute Press, 2004).

Figure 1.1
Major Combat Operations

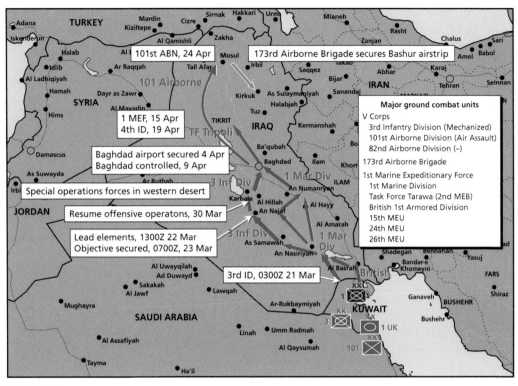

RAND *MG342-1.1*

ment and greater insight on which to base decisions to change logistics systems. In some cases the analysis supports the anecdotes; in others it will most likely provide new information about sustainment performance, its effects on operations, and the underpinning reasons for shortfalls. A series of RAND Arroyo Center reports will provide greater analytic depth on many of the issues discussed in this report.[4]

Sustainment Performance in OIF

By many performance measures, sustainment processes in OIF did not perform as well as desired for classes of supply other than fuel, with problems with spare parts and other items ordered "on demand" extending from combat operations well into

_____

[4] Reports will be published on battlefield logistics and effects on operations; spare parts demand analysis and deployed authorized stockage lists (ASL); Army Prepositioned Stock (APS) ASLs; APS war reserve secondary item inventory in CONUS and forward positioned; determining and resourcing national-level spare part requirements; and end-to-end distribution.

stability operations. Ensuring adequate fuel supply and distribution capabilities to enable a rapid advance to Baghdad was considered crucial, and this was reflected in mobilization and deployment decisions, theater preparation and resource decisions, and the fine tuning and practice of battlefield fuel resupply plans. And fuel had the natural advantage of a basically unlimited local source of supply, confining the supply chain to theater only and eliminating the purchase of raw materiel as a bottleneck, which simplified supply chain integration. As a result, units were well supported with fuel, with conditions across the fuel supply chain generally meeting expectations.

In contrast, insufficient theater distribution capacity and other factors, such as marked changes in plans that increased the demand for cargo trucks, first delayed and then limited the distribution of food and water to units during combat operations and all but prevented any spare parts deliveries from the start of ground combat until the fall of Baghdad. Spare parts then began to flow, but it took close to a year before the spare parts supply chain became effective. Ammunition resupply was often not as responsive as desired, and the preferred munitions were sometimes not available.

Early in OIF, tactical spare parts inventories at supply support activities (SSAs) in direct support of maneuver brigades and other groups of units were quickly depleted. In part this occurred as the result of supply chain disruptions, such as a lack of adequate communications equipment for automated part ordering during combat operations, and shipments sent to the wrong units. "Misshipments" declined in volume as time went on but remained an issue well into stability operations, caused by a misalignment between shipment preparation practices (specifically, consolidating shipments on pallets for air transport) in CONUS and theater distribution practices and capabilities. As stability operations led to very high, sustained demand that exceeded CONUS distribution center capacity,[5] strategic distribution times lengthened, further hindering both SSA performance and direct support from CONUS. Additionally, particularly during stability operations, demand rates were much higher for some parts than the rates used to set SSA inventory levels. Finally, as stability operations picked up in intensity in the summer of 2003, war reserves and the pace of the procurement surge proved insufficient to prevent the high demand rates from draining national spare part inventories of many items, leading to increasingly high rates of backordered materiel. With the combination of distribution problems, national supply problems, and high demand, SSAs were able to fill only one of every ten requests or so well into OIF, and direct support from CONUS to units for the remaining vast majority of requests suffered. For the 3rd Infantry Division's (ID) brigade combat teams (BCTs), issues with the design of the Army prepositioned stock (APS) SSAs in the brigade sets further hindered spares support.

___

[5] Distribution centers receive, store, and issue materiel provided by DoD suppliers and consolidate and prepare materiel for shipment.

Despite the sustainment shortfalls with respect to spare parts and other critical equipment supplies such as engine oil, units were able to maintain a high level of combat power for the month-long duration of major combat operations, albeit at a reduced standard of equipment readiness termed "shoot-move-communicate." However, even though the equipment readiness standard was lowered, soldiers and commanders report remaining confident in their equipment and, therefore, in their combat capability. Similarly, despite the distribution problems with food and water, which led to low on-hand levels during combat operations, and issues with the mix of munitions delivered, supplies and munitions remained sufficient to sustain the force and achieve desired combat effects, and commanders retained sufficient confidence in the logistics system to execute operations as planned.

Equipment readiness did degrade significantly during stability operations, for three reasons: first, deferred maintenance arising from the shift to a lower readiness standard steadily accumulated; second, sustainment performance problems continued; and third, the scope and intensity of Army operations following the fall of Baghdad expanded far beyond what had been anticipated, further increasing the demands for sustainment and outpacing the capacity of providers throughout the supply chain, extending back to the production base in the continental United States (CONUS). Within a week or so after the fall of Baghdad, the 3rd ID's reported equipment readiness dropped from about 90 percent for key ground combat systems to under 70 percent due to continuing distribution problems and a switch from the shoot-move-communicate standard to something closer to the traditional technical manual standard. Across V Corps, all combat systems fell below 80 percent readiness by early July.[6] The very heavily worked distribution assets, which include materiel-handling equipment such as forklifts and trucks, started showing signs of stress earlier, with many falling below 75 percent.[7]

What were the operational effects of the sustainment performance? Based upon wide-ranging interviews, after action reports, and other available accounts, we conclude that there were no major operational effects. That is, we have not been able to find evidence of an inability to accomplish a tactical mission, a failure to achieve desired battlefield effects, a change in an operational course of action related to these problems, or the foreclosure of a desired option stemming from a problem with sustainment processes. What the problems did affect were assessments of risk. The combination of low supply levels, known distribution problems, and limited visibility of incoming supplies resulted in calculations of elevated risk in the minds of the commanders and soldiers engaged in combat operations. By traditional standards and when supply status was viewed against expectations, supply risk sometimes appeared

---

[6] 14 July 3rd COSCOM readiness briefing.

[7] Ibid.

high, triggering some examination of whether the plan should be modified. But it seems that in the context of the situation, the risk was not high enough to demand a change in the plan.

We particularly analyzed the causes for the frequently cited pause in offensive momentum from 24 March 2003, when An Najaf was taken by the 3rd ID, until 31 March. We conclude that this pause was due to factors other than sustainment *process* problems or concerns, most notably the unexpected need to secure supply lines and the cities astride them. Iraqi paramilitary or *Fedayeen* became an unexpectedly strong threat to the lines of communication (LOCs), and As Samawah and An Najaf could not be bypassed as originally planned because doing so would have left these cities as places of safe refuge for the *Fedayeen* in close proximity to V Corps supply lines. Initially, the 3rd ID had to execute this unanticipated mission. It isolated An Najaf and provided LOC security, especially around As Samawah, until additional forces could be brought into Iraq to relieve it. As a result of the devastating sandstorm from 24 to 26 March and the time it took the 82nd Airborne Division and the 101st Airborne Division (Air Assault) to finish preparations for combat and move into positions, the 3rd ID was not able to complete its repositioning for the continued advance to Baghdad until 30 March.

Even though the potential operational effects of sustainment problems were successfully mitigated in OIF, this was accomplished through intensive management, creative adaptations, and soldiers continually pushing themselves to the limit, and such actions may not be enough to overcome such problems in every situation. Even so, risk was clearly elevated above commanders' and troops' comfort levels, and this level of risk might have triggered more significant changes in courses of action in the face of a more capable enemy. Similarly, even when subsistence requirements were met, the level of sustainment did not meet soldier expectations, from senior commanders to privates. Second, questions have been raised about how much longer the 3rd ID could have continued to be effective in high-intensity combat operations given the state of its equipment. Moreover, this equipment, which drew upon a substantial portion of the U.S. Army's prepositioned materiel, including all of the afloat assets, almost certainly would not have been a viable option for another immediate contingency operation, a need implied by the national strategy of "10-30-30."[8]

Thus, analysis of sustainment in OIF is important to help the Army derive critical lessons for producing a more effective joint logistics system. Additionally, the supply disruptions that occurred, the risk that arose, the readiness standards applied, the large forces needed to secure the LOCs, and the process performance all have po-

---

[8] Secretary of Defense Donald Rumsfeld has set out objectives for structuring the deployment capabilities of the U.S. military. The objectives call for U.S. forces to be able to deploy within 10 days, defeat an enemy within 30 days, and then be ready for another contingency within 30 days (see William Hawkins, "Speed and Power: Complements, Not Substitutes," *Army Magazine*, June 2004). An alternative for another contingency would have been to draw on the 3rd ID's home station equipment.

tential implications for future force operational and support concepts. For example, decisions about acceptable levels of risk and readiness standards are important for determining future force resource requirements. Further, an examination of OIF sustainment also has implications for the requirements determination and resourcing processes both in deliberate planning and in the run-up to an emerging contingency, particularly with regard to the consideration of stability and support operations after the conclusion of major combat operations.

In this report we describe the performance of the logistics system in sustaining Army forces through the provision of supplies necessary to conduct operations, the resulting sustainment effectiveness, and consequent effects on operations; provide detailed recommendations for improvement of the logistics system with respect to sustainment; and close with some questions raised by OIF sustainment that should be explored by the Army and others as future forces and plans are developed.[9]

A Joint Supply Chain Vision

We present our analyses and detailed recommendations within the context of a recommended model for a joint, interagency, fully integrated supply chain model for military logistics that focuses primarily on meeting the readiness needs of units in the field and secondarily on doing this as efficiently as possible.[10] The schematic in Figure 1.2 lays out the major elements of the supply chain with basic principles that can be applied to any military supply commodity. As the principles and the specific

---

[9] "Military logistics" in its broad sense and as typically used covers all activities to move, maintain, and provision forces, which includes the deployment of forces, the acquisition of materiel, and the sustainment of forces. Given this broad definition, logistics certainly had an effect on operational plans, most notably due to the foreclosure of the northern option for the introduction of heavy, armored forces from Turkey into Iraq. Issues with the ability of acquisition processes to meet emergent equipment requirements have been reported as well, in particular with respect to soldier safety. Within the field of logistics, sustainment is defined as the provision of goods and services to maintain the readiness of equipment and soldiers, to include health services, personnel services, other services, and the maintenance and supply of materiel. This report is limited to materiel sustainment, not including the provisioning or acquisition of new materiel to meet emergent requirements. Additionally, it focuses on the sustainment of Army forces, which encompasses the contributions of joint providers, not just Army logistics forces. Similarly, this research does not encompass all of the sustainment responsibilities of Army logistics forces, which provide support to joint and coalition forces. In particular, we have not examined the sustainment, including the contribution of Army units, of Marine Corps and other coalition ground forces.

[10] Developing an integrated supply chain is one of the four focus areas identified by the Army's Deputy Chief of Staff, G-4, that require high-priority efforts to improve logistics for a joint and expeditionary Army. A 2003 Army white paper lists these areas as follows: connect army logisticians, modernize theater distribution, improve force reception, and integrate the supply chain (Deputy Chief of Staff, G-4, Headquarters, Department of the Army, "Delivering Materiel Readiness to the Army," Army Logistics White Paper, December 2003). For more information on the supply chain initiatives, see Deputy Chief of Staff, G-4, Headquarters, Department of the Army, "Integrate the Supply Chain," Army Logistics White Paper, October 2004.

Figure 1.2
A Joint Supply Chain Vision to Align Organizations and Processes

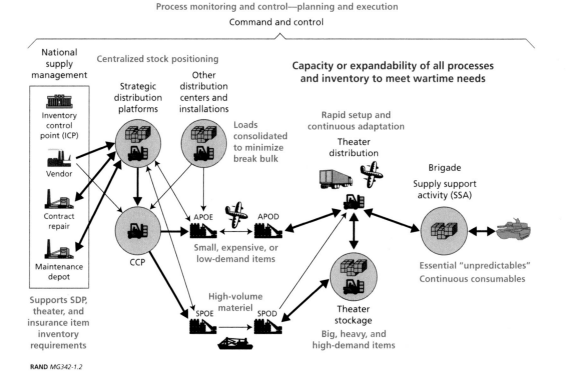

RAND *MG342-1.2*

characteristics of each commodity type are combined, different supply chain solutions will result, creating what appear to be distinct, commodity-based supply chains that share nodes and channels.

Tactical Supply Operations

The right side of Figure 1.2 depicts the generation of demands by tactical units and their direct support tactical supply operations, specifically the SSAs that hold inventory for brigades and other similar-sized units. For strategic and tactical mobility, the Army aims to minimize the storage capacity within tactical formations subject to having enough inventory capacity to sustain readiness. This mobility constraint, along with the capabilities of the rest of the system, has implications for both the range of items stored and how much of each is kept. To minimize needed capacity, storage space should be targeted primarily for items that are needed immediately upon demand or virtually continuously. This includes spare parts that drive readiness, food, water, fuel, medical supplies, ammunition, oil and other lubricants for equipment, limited amounts of materiel for the construction of defensive positions, and other basic subsistence items. It does not include items for which demand fulfillment can be temporarily delayed, such as noncritical spare parts or clothing, or items whose use can be scheduled. The latter encompasses parts for scheduled services that include events such as full track replacement, the periodic delivery of sundry packs with personal care items, construction materiel for relatively fixed facilities, and other items.

From a depth or quantity standpoint, the aim should be to have enough of each stocked item to avoid running out under a realistic set of assumptions that provides a margin of safety. The basic level should represent the quantity needed between anticipated wartime replenishment cycles and to cover at least short disruptions in resupply. The relative quantity needed varies substantially among commodity types, depending upon the nature of demand patterns or, in other words, demand variability and uncertainty. For example, it is safe to assume that each person will eat a specified number of meals each day and accordingly "push" out supplies to cover expected consumption on a regular basis, greatly limiting the amount of food that must be held by units. There is no need to wait for a meal to be consumed before starting the next one on its way. In contrast, some spare parts have tremendously variable demands, and there are literally tens of thousands of different parts that a maneuver brigade might need. So for some critical items, replenishment cannot reasonably be initiated until a demand occurs, increasing the effective time between replenishment cycles, and the unit needs to carry enough of these items to protect for "peak" demands up to a desired level, such as an intense week of combat. In practice for actual operations, the problem often becomes less about determining the minimum amount of supplies and storage capacity needed than about making the most effective utilization of relatively fixed, limited capacity. Unless augmentation is available and approved, each unit must be able to fit supplies within the storage capacity it can carry on its own transportation assets as authorized in modified tables of organization and equipment (MTO&E). So this tradeoff between readiness and the needed transportation assets to move supplies must be well treated in the force design process to determine the "right" level of lift capacity organic to a unit, and it must also be effectively considered in the deployment planning process in the event that operational parameters are expected to diverge substantially from those for which a unit was designed, which could require augmentation for the specific operation. For example, if a plan calls for the first resupply after five days and the unit was constructed with only enough carrying capacity to take three days of supplies, it will need additional trucks and trailers.

To keep the system working well, tactical supply organizations must be able to communicate their supply status, understand what is in the pipeline to them, and order items on demand or to replenish inventory.

Theater Distribution

Represented to the left of the brigade in Figure 1.2, theater distribution is the link between national providers and inventory, theater inventory, and units in the field. It consists of one or more distribution centers to receive materiel that comes into the theater and transload it for delivery to a unit or send it to a warehouse for storage. Distribution centers combine materiel being sent to units from different sources and prepare convoys for ground shipment or send it to an aerial port for intratheater air delivery. They link strategic transportation to theater transportation channels.

Developing and managing theater distribution is a complex task. For a contingency operation, the theater distribution system must often start from scratch and continually adjust to the amount, type, and location of forces to be supported as well as the varying types of needs that arise in different phases of an operation. This requires a well-planned and flexible choreography to maintain adequate distribution center capacities and theater transportation capacity, balanced across echelons, to keep supplies flowing reliably. Reliable flows also depend upon adequate supply line security and force protection capabilities, which has resource implications. To avoid developing early backlogs and shortages that are hard to dig out from, distribution center and transportation system setup should be rapid and appropriately phased within the deployment flow.

A second type of requirement is the ability to provide nearly instantaneous emergency response. There can be cases where unique battlefield circumstances quickly and unexpectedly deplete essential supplies, with demand continuing to loom. In particular, this can occur with ammunition during heavy, unexpected fights, creating critical spot shortages. Very rapid transportation assets, such as helicopters, can be used to handle these situations.

Strategic Distribution

What is often termed strategic distribution consists of two major sets of activities: preparing materiel for shipment and moving it overseas.[11] In describing the requirements for the sustainment of the Army and other joint and coalition forces today, it is useful to start with a look at the theater structure and the unique needs of distributing to a developing theater. With respect to the Army, the ends of the distribution system are individual soldiers, vehicles, and small units connected to small hubs or SSAs, which may be distributed across a theater. Especially early in an operation, there may be limited entry points for sustainment flow into the theater from which trucks or tactical aircraft will have to deliver supplies to the hubs. So from one or more central points, materiel needs to be sorted and consolidated for delivery to a

---

[11] For an overview of strategic distribution and its performance in OEF, see Marc Robbins et al., *The Strategic Distribution System in Support of Operation Enduring Freedom*, Santa Monica, CA: RAND Corporation, DB-428-USTC/DLA, 2004 (http://www.rand.org/publications/DB/DB428/).

SSA. However, the central theater distribution hubs may be new as well, without the sorting equipment and automation typical of fixed facilities. Additionally, distribution resources have to compete with other unit types, such as combat units, for their place in the deployment flow, making it valuable from a combat power buildup perspective to find ways to accomplish this mission without an early flow of large amounts of personnel and equipment resources. As a result, it makes sense to consolidate loads to the extent possible at permanent, fixed facilities in CONUS or other places where the United States has fairly robust, permanent infrastructure.[12]

Consolidating or building loads to the SSA level in CONUS supports the seamless delivery of materiel from distribution centers to SSAs with limited delay en route. No stops are necessary to break down, resort, and repackage loads. Rather, loads can be transloaded from one mode of transportation to another. The better the consolidation of materiel on pallets and in containers is synchronized with transportation, and the better transportation flows are coordinated across modes and nodes, the faster this flow will be. Tightly scheduling and coordinating when loads are "capped" and released for shipment, when trucks run from a warehouse to a port, when planes leave each day, when ships leave port, and so on enables effective synchronization. Positioning inventory at the start point of scheduled transportation where loads are consolidated for overseas shipment is the final step to achieving maximum velocity.[13]

The Department of Defense (DoD) strategic distribution system faces a unique challenge: highly variable and, more uniquely, sometimes virtually unpredictable large changes in demand in a very short period. Additionally, such large changes in demand occur very, very infrequently. Meeting this challenge requires the ability to rapidly and adequately increase the capacity of warehouses, load consolidation points, ports and other transshipment points, and transportation.

The Defense Logistics Agency (DLA) and U.S. Transportation Command (USTRANSCOM) have moved very close to this vision in support of the Army. Inventory has been concentrated in two strategic distribution platforms (SDPs) on the east and west coasts of the United States to support forces worldwide in their respective geographical areas of responsibility. These SDPs closely coordinate with air and sea ports on their respective coasts, and load consolidation centers collocated with the SDPs build loads for overseas shipment.

---

[12] This paradigm also applies to the Marine Corps and other forces deployed in hostile areas. The primary difference would be in the level of consolidation, which needs to be aligned with the respective organizational structures, such as where the lowest-level distribution hub is located in the force structure.

[13] Mark Y. D. Wang, *Accelerated Logistics: Streamlining the Army's Supply Chain,* Santa Monica, CA: RAND Corporation, MR-1140-A, 2000.

Theater General Support Stockage

For many items, it makes sense to store them in CONUS and send them directly from CONUS to SSAs upon demand; this is true, for instance, with regard to small, expensive items such as circuit cards. For other materiel and depending upon the situation, it is beneficial to establish relatively deep general support (GS) theater stockage and replenish it chiefly by sealift. The benefits of this strategy are that it frees constrained, high-value airlift for critical missions, and it reduces sustainment cost.

At a minimum, two general types of items should be forward positioned to minimize the reliance on airlift for sustainment. The first type consists of items with large, smooth demands: those items that continuously get consumed and generate large volume regardless of weight and size. Food is the primary example. The other type consists of big, heavy items, unless they are very expensive, which would drive up the cost of forward inventory. The items with a high ratio of shipping cost to purchase cost that makes it cost-effective to increase worldwide inventory to support surface replenishment include construction materiel, ammunition, some spare parts such as track, and other items such as tents. From a sustainment standpoint, this preserves airlift for lower-demand, smaller items; expensive items; and emergency missions.

There can be cases, though, in which it makes sense to also position critical readiness drivers that are large and expensive forward in theater inventory. Engines are an example. There are times when units cannot carry as many as they would like to support readiness, because they have limited mobile storage capacity. If the GS theater inventory can get parts to units significantly faster than CONUS sources can, then positioning these items in theater inventory would improve support effectiveness. However, this will not always be the case. If the strategic distribution system is working well, it should provide supplies almost as fast as a theater system, and in some cases it might do better.[14]

Small readiness drivers, especially inexpensive items, do not typically merit centralized forward positioning, because units themselves can generally carry sufficient stocks of such items for most situations without impeding mobility or requiring significant investment, negating the need for centralized theater inventory to compensate for thin unit stocks as might sometimes be the case with big, heavy items. Additionally, the amount of airlift consumed by these items is almost negligible. However, depending upon the constraints of a specific contingency operation and

---

[14] For most of OIF, even when strategic distribution was not working as well as it should, it still outperformed theater distribution. As both improved, the times for distribution from CONUS and theater GS inventory converged. It should also be noted that there is increasing delivery directly from CONUS to distributed deployed locations that bypass theater hubs.

the risk of strategic distribution being disrupted, the smaller, less-expensive readiness drivers could be considered for inclusion as well.

Upon initiation of a contingency, the Army and its supply chain partners should be prepared to establish this type of theater inventory.[15] Its establishment can be facilitated by prepositioned forward stocks in accordance with current practices. It also requires effective planning tools and units ready to deploy and execute the theater warehouse mission.

National Supply Management

National supply must have enough inventory to meet wartime demands until production can increase deliveries as needed and to fill the distribution pipelines that have been described. In particular, if theater stockage of big, heavy items is to be effective, there must be enough inventory of these items to fill the relatively long ocean shipment pipeline and to still have sufficient on-hand stock in CONUS to immediately satisfy critical demands by air, as necessary, during the time in which supplies are en route by ship. Achieving this level of inventory support requires effectively structured and resourced war reserves and agile "surge" processes. These processes span estimating the requirements to support a contingency, gaining approval to order some supplies in advance of operations, and the actual production of supplies by Army arsenals and maintenance depots and private-sector firms in the Army's industrial base.

Command and Control

The final crucial element of an effective and efficient supply chain is joint command and control (C2) to ensure that the various organizations spanning the various supply chains for the different commodity classes remain integrated and focused on the common objective of providing the best overall support possible—not necessarily the "best" segment performance of any one portion of a supply chain. "Best" is in quotation marks because one might often think that a distribution process segment achieving the minimum possible time is functioning at its best. But this is not the case if its practices are causing downstream problems. So one thing C2 must do is integrate planning so that each organization of the supply chain knows precisely what its suppliers are doing and what its customers expect. If one organization plans while using incorrect assumptions about the practices of another supply chain organization, serious problems can develop. For example, if war reserve requirements and funding are based upon incorrect assumptions about production base response capabilities, then there could be a gap in support.

---

[15] It should be noted that these principles apply to peacetime operations as well. Thus, DLA has established forward distribution centers in Germany and Korea to reduce shipping costs. Similarly, with operations continuing in Iraq, a new DLA distribution center has been opened in Kuwait.

Second, once a plan is developed, process monitoring and control is crucial for ensuring that it works well. Problems need to be identified and corrected as soon as possible. This requires good data transformed into effective information for personnel who are able to quickly correct a problem or drive a change in the appropriate portion of the supply chain.

Third, the information also enables the managers of the supply chain to use assets efficiently, and fourth, this information is crucial to good situational awareness. Situational awareness enables commanders and planners to realize when the plan should change and a different course of action should be pursued. In this vein, logistics situational awareness could potentially affect operational and even strategic decisionmaking in addition to enabling more effective support within a broader operational plan.

The OIF Supply Chain

In describing the supply chain that has supported OIF, we go through each of the elements of the system just described, starting this time at the national level and working toward the tactical units in the field. This description describes the primary elements and flows, not every organization and flow in the system. The procurement, repair, and inventory of spare parts and other subsistence items are managed by three organizations—DLA, Army Materiel Command (AMC), and the General Services Agency (GSA)—as indicated in Figure 1.3, which lays out organizational responsibilities and capability providers across the supply chain. DLA handles common items such as fuel, food, construction materiel, uniforms, and a wide range of "consumable" spare parts. AMC manages ammunition and weapon system or end item–specific spare parts such as engines. GSA manages common government items such as office supplies. In some cases, they have contracts with suppliers to provide materiel directly to ordering organizations, but for most items, these organizations own inventory stored in defense distribution centers operated by DLA as well as distribution centers managed by GSA.

The east coast SDP, which supports U.S. Central Command (CENTCOM), is Defense Distribution Depot Susquehanna, Pennsylvania (DDSP) near Harrisburg, as indicated on Figure 1.4, which shows the actual locations of primary distribution nodes in the OIF supply chain with respect to the sustainment of Army units. It has been the primary warehouse site for inventory used in support of OIF, and its collocated consolidation and containerization point (CCP) has integrated materiel from other DLA and GSA distribution centers as well as direct shipments from suppliers for consolidation on pallets and in containers. From the CCP, pallets have been trucked to either Charleston or Dover Air Force Bases, the primary aerial ports of

Figure 1.3
Organizational Responsibilities and Capability Providers in the Joint Supply Chain

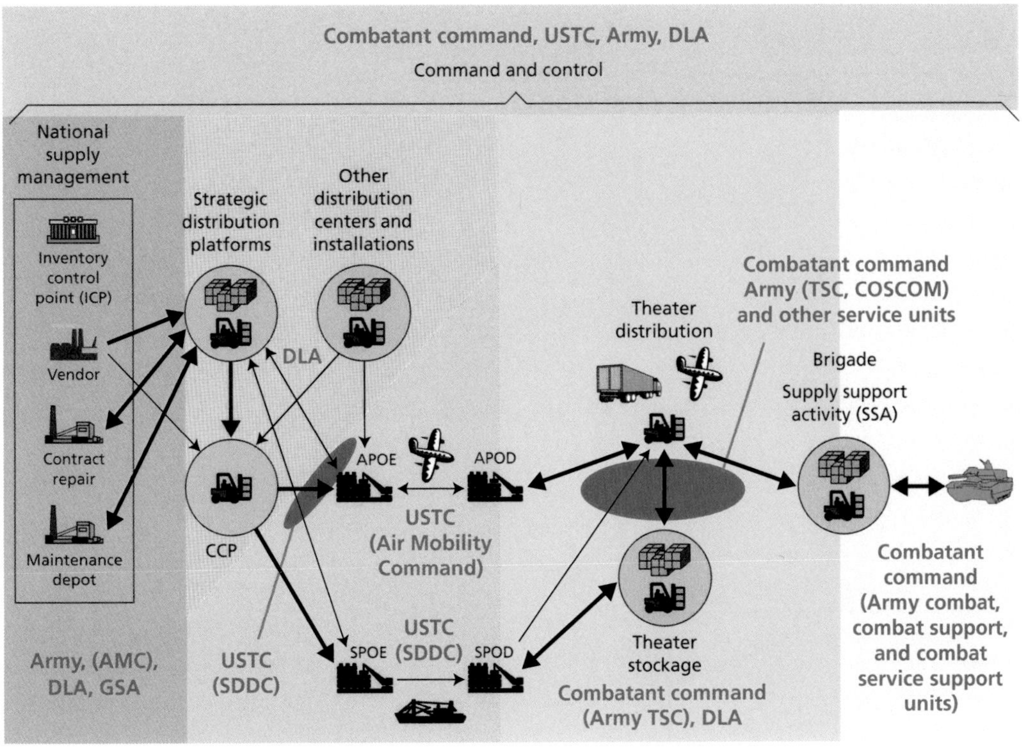

RAND *MG342-1.3*

embarkation (APOEs) for the sustainment of OIF, to be loaded on either military aircraft or commercial cargo plans chartered by Air Mobility Command. As discussed in the report, some materiel, such as hazardous items, is sent directly to APOEs for consolidation on pallets. Containers have been trucked to either Norfolk or Newark, New Jersey, to be loaded onto commercial container ships.

Prior to, during, and for a short period after major combat operations, most sustainment materiel was sent from CONUS to Kuwait, primarily through Kuwait City International Airport with aerial port operations conducted by Air Mobility Command, or the seaport of Ash Shuwaykh operated by Army units under the Surface Distribution and Deployment Command (SDDC) and the 377th Theater Support Command (TSC), both indicated on Figure 1.4.[16] From the two ports, shipments were sent to the theater distribution center (TDC), under the 377th TSC, in Camp

---

[16] A major exception was the delivery of supplies to the 173rd Airborne Brigade in the Kirkuk area, which received materiel via airlift direct from supplies held in Europe.

Figure 1.4
Primary Nodes and Channels in the Strategic Distribution for OIF

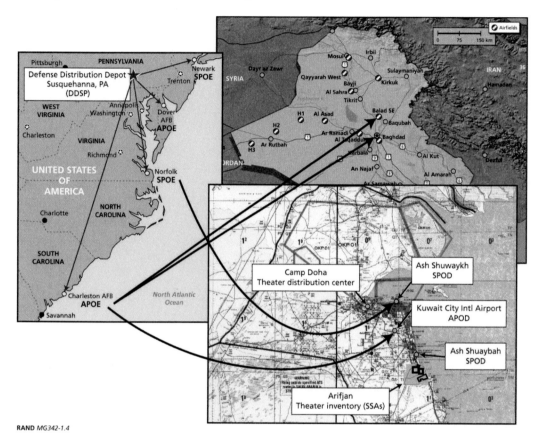

RAND *MG342-1.4*

Doha to be routed to the appropriate location, which could include either transloading for delivery directly to a unit or sending the materiel to one of several theater-level warehouses in Kuwait, also under the 377th TSC. When these warehouses then shipped materiel to units, they would send the materiel to the TDC. The TDC would then combine materiel from all sources and prepare convoys for deliveries to units. During major combat operations, for shipments to Army units, the TDC convoys would hand off their materiel to V Corps' 1st Corps Support Command (COSCOM) in southern Iraq. The COSCOM was then responsible for deliveries to units, with convoy routings evolving as V Corps advanced and then as land forces extended the coalition's reach to Iraq's border to begin stabilizing the country. The initial zones of responsibility for stability and support operations are depicted in Figure 1.5.

After major combat operations, the 1st COSCOM quickly established Logistics Support Area Anaconda at the Balad air base north of Baghdad as a central hub for

Figure 1.5
Initial Zones of Responsibility for Stability and Support Operations With a Rough Depiction of Major Convoy Routes

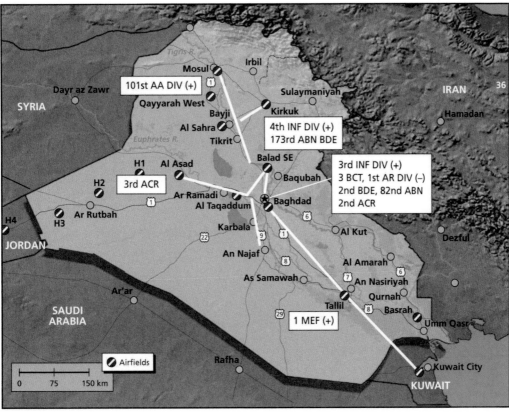

RAND MG342-1.5

SOURCE: V Corps, Department of the Army, "The Road to 'Victory!' in Operation Iraqi Freedom," briefing. Routes based on personal knowledge and adaptation from COL R.W. Olsen and MAJ T. Baker, "Theater MEDLOG Support Operations Overview," 23 May 2004.

support to units in the northern half of Iraq. This included the establishment of a corps distribution center (CDC). Once the CDC was established, the TDC generally sent convoys to the CDC, which would then send out convoys to the Army's major units in Iraq. Additionally, as the operation evolved, first Baghdad International Airport was opened to military cargo aircraft, and then in late 2003, Balad became a direct point of entry into the theater for sustainment cargo. As the theater has evolved the TDC has continued to operate, as ocean shipments must still arrive in Kuwait and the amount of inventory held in Kuwait has increased. The CDC combines materiel sent from the TDC and directly from CONUS (or the DLA distribution center in Germany) for delivery to units.

Other modes of transportation, including trucks from Germany and rail from the Iraqi seaport of Umm Qasr, have been used as well. However, this description covers the dominant transportation modes, transshipment locations, warehouses, and distribution centers employed to sustain Army units for much of OIF. As of the writing of this report, new inter- and intratheater air routes are increasingly being opened for delivery to major units around Iraq, bypassing the TDC and the CDC.

Organization of This Report

In Chapters Two through Six, we describe the performance of each of these elements of the supply chain, identify which of the key elements in Figure 1.1 did not perform well, examine the causes of shortfalls, and offer recommendations. Chapter Seven offers some potential implications for future force development that should be explored and discusses overall lessons learned or key issues to be addressed across the supply chain. More detailed analyses are available in companion reports devoted to the specific topics summarized here.

CHAPTER TWO

Tactical Supply Operations

The determination and resourcing of food, water, and fuel inventory levels at the tactical level in OIF should be considered relatively effective, with ammunition inventory determination somewhat less effective as a result of issues with the mix of munitions. There were enough of these commodities provided to combat units to enable them to make it through supply chain disruptions. The story for critical on-demand items, mostly spare parts and packaged petroleum, oil, and lubrication (POL) products, is much different, however. Thus, in this chapter on tactical supply, the focus is on the stockage of spare parts and the information systems needed to order them. The tactical supply performance of other items is treated in Chapter Three, which reports on theater distribution.

A Few Basic Army Inventory Metrics and Terms

To evaluate the effectiveness of tactical inventories and help diagnose the sources of any shortfalls in performance, several metrics are useful: accommodation, satisfaction, and fill rate. We use a simple example to explain the meanings of these metrics.

- **Accommodation.** Suppose you go to the auto parts store for ten different parts. You search the shelves and talk to a clerk and find out the store only carries six of them. Each of those six has a dedicated shelf space. The other four items always have to be ordered from a national warehouse. The accommodation "rate" is thus 60 percent or 6 of 10. Accommodation measures the quality of the breadth of inventory requirements: Are the "right" items being selected and authorized for stockage?

- **Satisfaction.** When you go to the six different shelves, you find that two of them are empty. The store has run out of two of the six items that you need and they typically carry. Thus, the satisfaction "rate" is 67 percent or 4 of 6. Satisfaction measures the quality of the depth or quantity of each item that is stocked: Are "enough" of the stocked items being carried to meet critical demands?

Figure 2.1
Key Tactical Supply Characteristics in the Joint Supply Chain Vision (see pages 8–9)

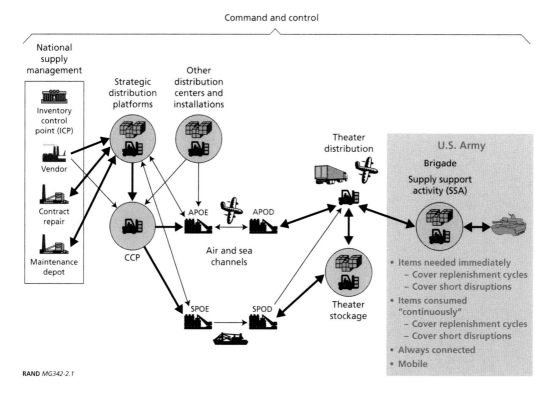

RAND *MG342-2.1*

- **Fill.** When you leave the store, you leave with 4 of the 10 parts you needed, for a fill "rate" of 40 percent. Fill rate is a total measure of inventory performance.

In the Army, the spare parts selected and then authorized for stockage at the brigade or an equivalent level make up what is called the authorized stockage list or ASL.[1] While nominally a list of items authorized for stock along with the authorized quantities (known as requisitions objectives or ROs) and reorder points (ROPs), the physical inventory itself is typically also called an ASL in the Army. Each maneuver brigade has a SSA assigned to it that manages and operates an ASL warehouse. The parts are selected to support the brigade as effectively as possible within the storage constraints of the mobile warehouse, which consists of trucks, trailers, and containers that ideally have well-laid-out storage aids such as cabinets to maximize their utility. All units in the Army receive their primary direct spare parts support from a SSA, whether units in a maneuver brigade, units under division control, or units in eche-lons above division. When organizations task organize, however, the supporting SSA

---

[1] The inventory held at installation level or by GS theater warehouses also forms an ASL.

can change, which is a problem if the new SSA did not previously support any units with similar equipment and thus does not have some of the requisite spare parts. This has tended to occur less for organic elements of maneuver brigades, such as mechanized infantry companies, than for other types of units. This issue may lessen to a degree as the Army adopts new, modular brigade combat team (BCT) units of action (UAs). In particular, what have been division-level assets will now be assigned to BCT UAs, so the BCT UA SSAs should be designed to support the wider range of equipment.

Prepositioned ASL Breadth: Did the Army Preposition the Right Parts?

To accelerate the deployment, the Army used prepositioned equipment for most of the 3rd ID. The three BCTs drew prepositioned brigade sets, which also include ASLs with parts matched to the equipment. None of the three ASLs performed very well, but the one ASL of the three that had been used for rotational training did better than the other two, which had never been exercised. Changes had been made to the ASL used in training by some of the units that had used it as they discovered problems over the course of exercises. In this report, we concentrate on the latter two ASLs.

While a couple of the vehicle types in the APS brigade sets that were drawn by the 3rd ID were different from the ones they had at home station at Fort Stewart and Fort Benning, most were the same, and even where variants differed, most parts were common across the vehicle variants. Despite this, the home station ASLs designed for deployments, but left at home with the brigades' equipment, had very little in common with the prepositioned ASLs. They were developed with different methodologies and using different data.

The Venn diagram in Figure 2.2 makes this design difference very clear. For example, the requirements for the APS ASL drawn by the 203rd Forward Support Battalion (FSB) supporting the 3rd BCT of the 3rd ID had 1,950 required parts that were not in the home station ASL, which had 1,920 parts not in the APS ASL requirements. The intersection of the two consisted of just 571 parts, of which 472 were actually on hand when the ASL was drawn by the 203rd FSB. Probably due to supply availability and budgetary constraints, the actual APS ASL drawn was missing some of the required parts, and it had a small number of parts not on the required list.

With records of the parts that 3rd BCT demanded in OIF, we could use those data to predict how well different ASLs would have met the demand. What we discovered was that the part mixes for the prepositioned ASLs were not well selected for the prepositioned equipment. Figure 2.3 compares the predicted performance for the

Figure 2.2
A Comparison of the Composition of the APS ASL Requirements, the Actual APS ASL, and the 203rd FSB's Home Station ASL in Terms of Different Parts

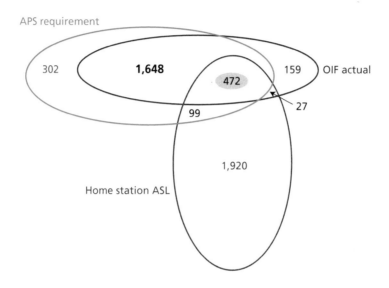

203rd FSB, 3rd BCT, 3rd ID

APS requirement

302   **1,648**   159   OIF actual

472

99   27

1,920

Home station ASL

203rd's required APS ASL with the predicted performance of its home station ASL using the actual OIF demand stream for the 3rd BCT. The left-hand set of bars shows that the predicted accommodation percentage for the home station ASL is 20 points higher than for the APS ASL requirements when considering all spare part requests. The right-hand set shows a similar difference when limiting the population of requests to readiness drivers, with the performance of both ASLs higher as they should be according to the supply chain vision.[2] The rightmost column in each set of three shows how the actual APS ASL performed, which was slightly worse than the required APS ASL. The APS ASL accommodated only about 25 percent of all spare part requests and, more important, only about one-third of requests for readiness drivers. Additionally, about two-thirds of the required and actual on-hand APS ASL parts were not demanded in OIF by the 3rd BCT. In contrast, this proportion is about one-third for the home station ASL.

Different methodologies and data sources were used to develop the APS and home station ASLs. The more critical difference appears to be the input data. APS

---

[2] Readiness drivers are those parts that maintainers must replace in order to restore a broken vehicle or weapon system, such as a tank, to mission-capable condition. Specifically, they are defined in this research as a list of parts generated from an archive of daily deadline reports, commonly called "O26" prints, submitted by active Army units.

Figure 2.3
Comparing Accommodation for the 203rd FSB's APS and Home Station ASLs

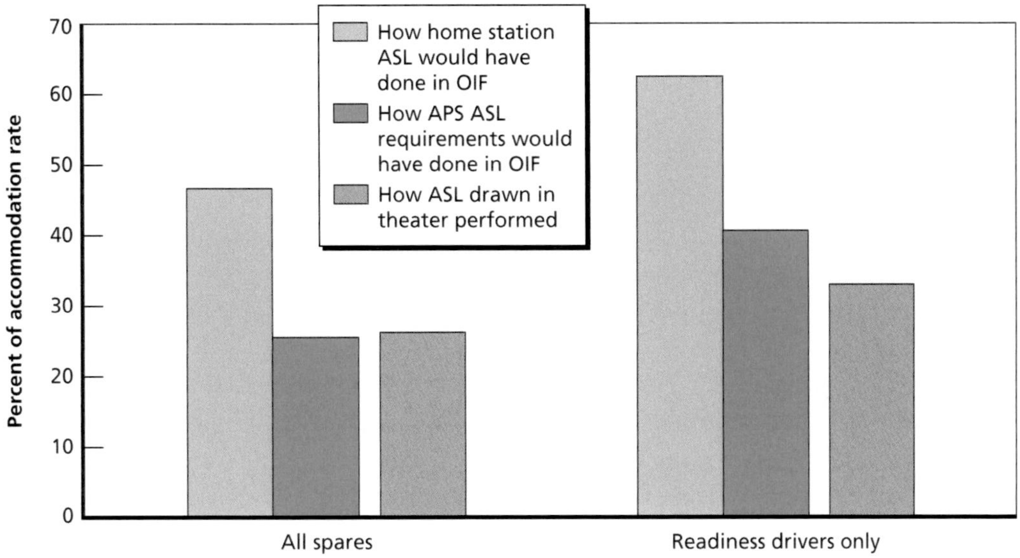

RAND MG342-2.3

ASLs were based upon what are called candidate items files (CIF) that have part-to-end-item mappings and estimated failure rates. Failure rates start as engineering estimates or proxy values, with some updates based upon empirical data. In contrast, home station ASLs are based solely on actual demand patterns for the units supported by a SSA. The definition of what is critical or a readiness driver in the APS ASLs is also extremely broad, including many parts that are never seen to "deadline" a system in the field.[3] Additionally, the APS ASL criteria exclude some parts that field experience has shown to be readiness drivers. Beyond the definition of which parts are critical, the APS ASL methodology also assumes that all critical parts, specifically those coded with essentiality code "C" or mission essential, contribute equally to readiness for their assigned system.[4]

---

[3] To deadline means to render a system not mission capable.

[4] Maintenance technicians across the Army often advance the proposition that the readiness contribution of parts is not equal. However, the Army's data has not been sufficient to examine this proposition in the past. Recently, the Army has begun centrally archiving parts requests for deadlined end items, with the requests linked to work orders. These data have been used to show that while 50 to 60 percent of the requests for deadlined tanks, for example, are for parts that cost less than $100, these parts only enable the completion of less than 10 percent of the deadlining work orders (i.e., inexpensive parts are often ordered in conjunction with a more expensive part, such as an engine, when an end item becomes not mission capable). The data also reveal that less than a third of the spare parts coded as critical (essentiality code of "C") that are demanded in a typical heavy BCT appear to deadline Army end items.

Along with the assumption about equal readiness contribution, which has been a product of insufficient data, there are other potential weaknesses in the data that could have contributed to the poor performance of the APS ASLs. First, it is difficult to estimate failure factors for very-low-demand items, particularly if the sample period is short (e.g., a demand that occurs in a two-week training exercise may not occur again for a year or more).[5] Finally, the methodology trades off parts based on the readiness benefit versus the cost. A methodology that used a mobility constraint or storage optimization may produce a somewhat different result, especially if storage location or bin size is correctly used for small parts instead of part dimensions.[6] Furthermore, items that can be stored in bins in cabinets or on shelves within vans or containers and items that require bulk storage (e.g., pallets on flatbed trailers) should not trade off against each other as they use different storage assets.

By contrast, the methodology used to develop the home station ASLs is based upon actual unit demands. While data problems still exist, they are almost certainly significantly less than those associated with the candidate items files and failure factors used to develop the APS ASLs. Also, the methodology establishes a demand floor: no parts with a very low demand will be authorized for stockage.[7] Hence, the items authorized for stockage are more likely to have recurring and more predictable demands.

Another problem besides poor part mix faced the 203rd FSB as it tried to use the prepositioned ASL. Rather than being given containers with warehouse locations to put on trucks and trailers, it was given containers full of parts, and its personnel had to build a warehouse on the fly. In this case, the operational consequences were minimal, because the unit had time to prepare for combat. This would not be the case in a rapid, expeditionary operation. Additionally, the information system used to account for APS ASLs is not fully compatible with the standard field system, which required manual intervention and led to information system problems, hampering operations.

---

[5] A recent analysis of demands at Fort Knox, home of the Army's Armor School, showed that of the parts with demands, almost 60 percent had two or fewer requests in two years. Of these 60 percent, almost 75 percent did not experience a demand in the following year. Samples taken during specific training events are likely to lead to overestimates of the failure rates of the low-failure parts that are demanded during the events. Conversely, some low-failure-rate parts will not show up at all, preventing the development of an accurate estimate of their failure rates.

[6] For example, a cost-minimization model would see a 500,000-to-1 ratio between a tank engine and a small one-dollar part. While the pure size ratio between the two may be similar, the effective size ratio is limited by the smallest available bin or shelf location. Thus, in this example, the ratio of storage size may be 125 cubic feet to 0.125 cubic feet (where 0.125 would be the bin size), or as low as 1,000-to-1.

[7] See Kenneth Girardini et al., *Dollar Cost Banding: A New Algorithm for Computing Inventory Levels for Army SSAs*, Santa Monica, CA: RAND Corporation, MG-128-A, 2004, for an explanation of the Army's ASL determination process and the algorithm employed.

Finally, ASLs are generally designed to be replenished as inventory is consumed. ROPs and ROs are established for each part to achieve a desired level of confidence of having the part when demanded in the most efficient manner possible. These parameters are based upon the demand rate, replenishment lead time, item price, and standard ordering and inventory holding costs. Only a single authorized level, as opposed to ROPs and ROs, were computed for the prepositioned ASLs. When APS ASLs were transferred to the field inventory management information system, the units had to develop and input ROPs and ROs for every stocked item during preparation for combat.

ASLs Deployed from CONUS Had Better Part Mixes

As seen in the discussion of the APS ASLs for the 3rd ID, home station accommodation rates for readiness drivers were relatively good. The question for many was whether they would hold up in OIF and other real-world operations, given that they were based upon home station training data. The answer is yes. Figure 2.4 shows that the accommodation rates for units that deployed with their home station ASLs were

Figure 2.4
Accommodation at Home Station (HS) for the Last Six Months Prior to Deployment and During OIF for the ASLs of Major Army Units

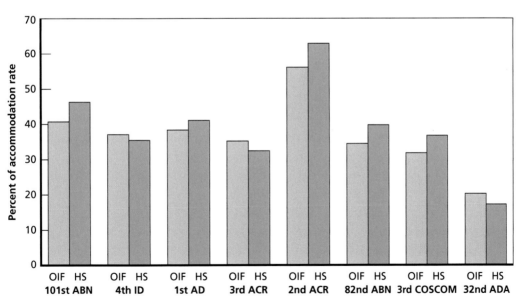

similar in OIF to the rates they experienced at home. This is because the mix of parts demanded by units in OIF was remarkably similar to what they demand at home. This result is seen consistently across different fleets. Thus, this supports the continued use of home station training data to select the mix of parts to stock for deployments.

OIF demand patterns further confirmed some home station demand patterns that have implications for Army ASL policy. We found that most major platform "families"—e.g., all HMMWV variants would be considered a family—require about 75 to 200 different parts to achieve good ASL performance that effectively supports readiness, depending upon the complexity of the family (number of variants) and the complexity of the platform (e.g., a M1 tank has more parts that affect field readiness than do other ground systems). A typical Army heavy BCT has about 20 different major families and another 14 or so less complex families requiring fewer parts. In total, about 150 different readiness-reportable systems require spare parts support within a BCT. So the number of different parts needed to effectively support even just the major systems in a BCT grows quickly. These simple facts have important implications for force design in terms of the number of different systems and the commonality of parts among them.

One might ask, however, about the one-third of home station ASL parts for the 203rd FSB that were not demanded by its supported BCT in OIF and wonder whether they should be stocked. Most Army ASLs support a wide breadth of fleets and other end items, many with only a small quantity. Thus, to support them well, many relatively low-demand parts are needed. To get enough breadth of parts to provide good readiness, the ASL selection process has to include many parts that will be demanded relatively infrequently, say twice per year. In some years, and even more in shorter periods, quite a few of these parts will not experience demands. We have found similar trends when examining home station ASLs and home station demands from year to year. Simply put, the greater the probability a unit wants of having the parts it may need in an operation, the more it will have to accept parts that, mostly by chance, are not needed during any specific operation or period. The decision becomes what balance to strike given the costs and risks. More parts can improve readiness but at a cost in terms of ASL size. Different optimization goals can be chosen: minimize inventory investment or minimize inventory storage footprint (to minimize mobility requirements) to achieve a required level of readiness.

Another important issue that OIF demand data confirmed is that an inventory model that only considers part demands will probably not perform as well as a more complex model that considers part demands as they pertain to the completion of maintenance work orders to correct equipment faults. Many faults require more than one part to fix. There may be a primary part, such as an alternator, and one or more companion parts, such as a bolt, seal, gasket, washer, belt, nut, etc. Without the primary part, the work order cannot be completed. What this means is that there are dependencies among parts that should be considered when determining what to stock, and thus not all parts that affect readiness do so equally. Just as in home station training, most parts needed for deadlining repairs in OIF were less than $100. But also just as in home station training, most work orders needed a relatively expensive part to be completed. So having lots of cheap parts in the ASLs is advised, but it is not sufficient to maintain a high level of equipment readiness.

A final issue arising with regard to part mixes in OIF has nothing to do with the types of parts demanded, the choice of inventory model, modeling assumptions, or input data: rather, it has to do with how ASLs are structured and the process by which they are constructed. ASL determination is generally a deliberate planning process, with careful review of the output by the maintainers and other logisticians in a unit. Then once decisions are made, parts have to be ordered and received, and the storage has to be reconfigured in accordance with changes in the mix and depth of parts selected for stockage. Additionally, the ASL is designed as a whole. That is, pieces cannot easily be broken off and sent with portions of a brigade or another supported set of units. This has implications on two levels.

In OIF, many support relationships changed, during both deployment planning and operations. Neither the more permanent changes in task organization made during deployment planning nor the dynamic task organizations during combat and other operations were reflected in ASL changes, sometimes impeding support to a unit. For example, a tank battalion task organized to a brigade from a light division in the midst of combat operations would have to be supported by a SSA without any parts for tanks, heavy recovery vehicles, and other tracked vehicles. Similarly, divisional units "sliced" to brigade combat teams would be supported by SSAs without parts for any unit equipment they might have, such as a Fox Nuclear, Biological, and Chemical Reconnaissance System. A construction unit assigned to be supported by a divisional main support battalion during deployment planning would be supported by a SSA without some parts needed to support its dump trucks, graders, and other unique equipment. These are actual examples from OIF. Task organization is much less of an issue with regard to the mix of parts held by a SSA when units become supported by a SSA that already supported other units with similar equipment—e.g., a tank battalion moving from one heavy BCT to another or a truck company moving from one corps support group to another.[8] One thing that should be clear from the examples is that a more responsive ASL change process could potentially handle deliberately planned task organizations such as the planned addition of an engineer group to the supported units of a main support battalion (MSB). However, dynamic battlefield task organization can probably only be supported by having parts move with the unit or already having the parts at the level of the organization that moved

---

[8] This type of task organization could affect the quantity requirement for each part. In cases in which the SSA has to support more of a given system but the part quantities are not changed, ASL satisfaction will go down.

from one BCT to another. Or maybe such "contingency" packages could be available in theater, as this is a severe problem only in the minority of situations in which a SSA receives a unit type with equipment it normally does not support.

It should be noted that the Army's current conversion to BCTs that include "permanent" ownership of what were often divisional pooled assets will probably reduce this task organization inventory adjustment problem somewhat. In particular, the type of within-division task organization that used to be common, with divisional assets to include signal, military intelligence, military police, and chemical reconnaissance now assigned to BCTs, will no longer be necessary. However, task organization between heavy and light brigade combat teams will still result in the same issues as in OIF. Additionally, sustainment units of action will have the challenge of potentially supporting different types of support units and possibly joint and multinational units.

ASLs Were Quickly Depleted

Many demands for spare parts were unmet in OIF even when the right parts had been authorized for stockage. This is because the supplies of these parts were quickly depleted. There were three reasons for this: the Army did not stock the ASLs to (1) wartime operating tempo, nor did it stock to cover (2) the long replenishment wait times and (3) supply disruptions experienced in OIF. The Army's ASL depths were computed based upon home station demands and replenishment times along with mobility and cost constraints. However, the demand levels for some parts were much higher than those experienced at home during training events, and the replenishment times were longer. Home station replenishment times were exceeded by factors of two and, in effect, sometimes more because some shipments were misdirected and never delivered to the ordering unit. In some cases, communications and information system problems delayed replenishment requests from even hitting the supply system. The resulting depleted shelves drove satisfaction rates for ASLs to very low levels, such as from 65 percent at home for the 101st Airborne Division to just 20 percent in OIF, as seen in Figure 2.5. Thus, fill rates became extremely low, often just 10 percent or even less, the realm in which an ASL becomes worth very little to sustaining equipment readiness. Almost every demand became a pass through to the national supply base in CONUS, thirty days away by air for significant portions of OIF, assuming the item was still available to ship. Some units, though, did have enough spare parts for the first couple weeks of the operation. So the depth would have been helpful for a short-notice, short-duration contingency or one in which combat operations requiring high readiness lasted only a couple of weeks—like OIF major combat operations. In fact, the 26th FSB ASL supporting the 2nd BCT of the

Figure 2.5
Inventory Performance at Home Station (HS) for the Last Six Months Prior to Deployment and During OIF for the ASLs of Major Army Units

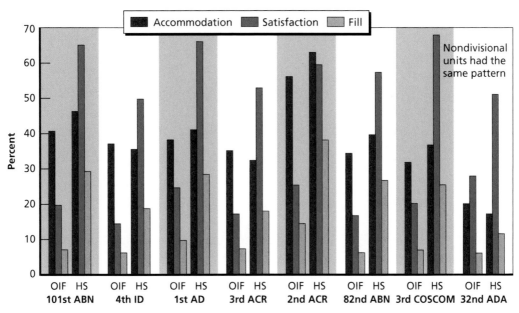

RAND *MG342-2.5*

3rd ID had enough of most major assemblies for tanks and Bradleys to get to Baghdad.[9] After that point, though, distribution problems and continued demand led to bare shelves.

Deployment practices, mobility constraints, and the existing ASL determination automation made it difficult for units to adjust depth appropriately before deploying and while conducting operations. When they deployed, units had to adopt new SSA address codes, requiring the resetting of computers and inventory management parameters. This decoupled their part-demand histories, which are critical for conducting ASL reviews to adjust an ASL's breadth and depth, from their new SSA address codes and inventory management parameters. This problem could be overcome by automatic replication or migration of a SSA's demand history data from the old SSA address code to the new one in the Army's supply information system. Additionally, the current algorithm programmed in the Army's systems is designed to employ two years of demand history. Thus, ASL recommendations from the existing implementation of the algorithm during the first few months in theater would react to the higher demands, but since they would also be based upon prior home station

---

[9] It drew the prepositioned ASL used for training in Kuwait, and the 26th FSB had time to augment the ASL as the 2nd BCT deployed to Kuwait in September 2002.

demands (or no prior demands if the history were not transferred), the recommendations might not reflect theater requirements appropriately. Accordingly, the algorithm should be adjusted to compensate for the shorter time period, which could be applied to the existing automation. Finally, we have found that most ASLs in the Army are at their mobility constraints for bulk storage used for items such as engines. Some room is available, though, in many SSAs for increased depth of small items stored in cabinets. Storage limitations combined with the difficulties of reconfiguring a warehouse while preparing to deploy are actually the biggest long-term impediments to rapid ASL adjustment for deployments. A partial solution to this is closer alignment of ASLs at home station with deployed depth needs based upon likely contingency replenishment time and demand rates.

Part Ordering During Combat Operations

Current ASLs and the models used to determine them assume that when parts are consumed from the ASL, the SSA will immediately order a replenishment when the appropriate level or the reorder point (ROP) is reached (usually after each order for expensive items) or will immediately order each nonstocked item from the supply chain when needed to complete a repair. For a variety of reasons, these assumptions did not hold during OIF's major combat operations. Very few parts were ordered during this period. This is a concern because any delays before ordering extend the replenishment time beyond the typical requisition wait time, which is often used to plan ASL depth. As we explain in the chapters on theater and strategic distribution, even if more parts had been ordered from the national system (either to replenish ASLs or to correct a specific fault) during the period of major combat operations, they probably still would not have arrived when expected and certainly not during combat operations. Nevertheless, it is important to understand the reasons why units were unable to order during combat operations in OIF so that this capability shortfall can be remedied in future contingencies, particularly those with longer major combat periods.[10]

The lack of ordering stems from issues at two levels: creating a request and submitting a requisition. An analogy would be your physician first diagnosing your illness and writing out a prescription and then calling it in to your local pharmacy; another analogy is filling out an order on Amazon.com and clicking the send button. Similarly, the first step in ordering a part is for a maintainer to diagnose the problem, write it down, and give it to a supply clerk to create a part request, which is sent to

---

[10] Improved communications is a critical part of the Deputy Chief of Staff, G-4's "connect Army logisticians" focus area. See Deputy Chief of Staff, G-4, Headquarters Department of the Army, "Connect Army Logisticians," Army Logistics White Paper, October 2004.

the SSA. The time series in Figure 2.6 represented by the red line shows maintenance requests by day for the 1st BCT of the 3rd ID. Note the relatively heavy activity in February and the first half of March 2003, followed by relatively little activity from the time the BCT moved to the border with Iraq in mid-March until the fall of Baghdad in early to mid-April. Then requests picked up again. Note also the complete absence of ordering for the first few days of combat operations when the BCT was advancing from Kuwait to An Najaf. There was no intent and basically little feasibility of ordering parts given current maintenance systems during this period of intense activity with nearly constant movement. Ordering picked up somewhat for a few days as the advance, but not combat, paused from 24 to 30 March. The conditions limited ordering to only the most critical requests, far below what might be ordered in a more garrison-like environment. Then requests slowed again as the brigade maneuvered and fought from Karbala to Baghdad.

Now note the blue line, which reflects daily requisitions submitted from the SSA to the remainder of the supply chain. It reflects a nearly total blackout of non-line-of-sight communications capability for SSA supply systems during major combat operations. Lacking mobile satellite communications, the 3rd ID and other units

Figure 2.6
Maintenance Requests by 1st BCT, 3rd ID Units (document dates) and 3rd FSB, 1st BCT, 3rd ID Requisitions (established date)

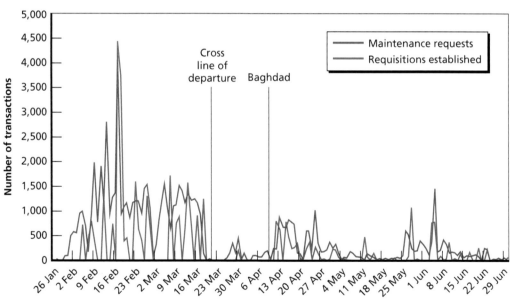

could not order parts on a distributed battlefield with extended supply lines and frequent movement. The SSAs lacked adequate communications capability. This is a contributor to the reduced rate of part request generation by maintenance in the second portion of combat operations. Once some units realized that parts could not be ordered and ASLs did not have the right parts, there was little reason to create part requests.

Recommendations

SSAs

- Ensure that SSA warehouse capacities, as defined by the number and types of trucks and trailers authorized in SSA tables of organization and equipment (TO&Es) to carry ASL containers, are sufficient to meet readiness needs through standardized, detailed readiness and capacity tradeoff analyses.
  - SSA TO&E designs should be based upon a standard, detailed readiness analysis during the force development process. The needed capacity should consider the number and depth of parts needed to support all end items. In recent years, the degree of analytic rigor used to develop SSA TO&Es has varied substantially.
  - Consider TO&E revisions for current and planned units as necessary to meet support goals.
  - SSA TO&Es should include storage aids, such as cabinets, to permit units to make more consistent and effective utilization of available storage capacity. Currently, storage aid decisions are made and funded locally, leading to widely varying effective capacity for similar TO&Es.

APS ASLs

- Improve input data quality and modify the methodology used to determine APS ASL requirements to leverage additional and improved data sources.[11]
  - Employ empirically based input data to the extent possible.
    - To help identify the spare parts that drive equipment readiness, the Army should use field readiness data as archived in the equipment downtime analyzer (EDA). These data are more effective for determining critical

---

[11] RAND Arroyo Center has worked with AMC to develop a new APS ASL methodology based upon these recommendations. The methodology makes use of an archive of parts that units in the field have reported as deadlining their equipment during operations and is currently being used to develop new requirements for APS ASLs.

parts in a field environment than are essentiality codes, and they permit readiness driver identification by model.[12]

- ◆ Limit the ASL to EDA parts for reportable (major) systems, and supplement these parts with high-demand parts associated with nonreportable end items that are not included in unit readiness reports.

- ◆ To establish the depth for each item, the Army should either rely on the actual demand histories of units with similar end item quantities to those in the APS equipment sets or develop improved, Army-wide failure factors based on periods of high operating tempo.

- – Modify the APS ASL methodology to focus on achieving equipment readiness goals through the effective use of storage capacity.

  - ◆ The linkage to readiness should be based on the contribution of inventory to work order completion rather than the percentage of part requests filled. This brings the dependencies among parts needed to complete repairs into consideration in the stockage determination process.

  - ◆ Storage capacity should be treated as a constraint (if the number of trucks and trailers is considered as a given) or as an objective (if storage capacity can be flexible). In the latter case, storage capacity would be minimized to meet the readiness objectives. If readiness objectives can be met within storage constraints, the methodology can be used to determine the potential for storage capacity reduction or, instead, to minimize investment cost to meet the readiness goal.

  - ◆ When using a storage capacity constraint, the Army should base storage requirements for parts on the minimum required storage location sizes, not item sizes. Regardless of how small a part is, it still consumes the smallest accessible bin size. Also, separate constraints should be established for items that can be stored in bins versus those that require "bulk storage" space such as on a flatbed trailer. Parts that are difficult to store in a mobile warehouse should be excluded by using parameter files that are currently embedded within the dollar cost banding module within the Integrated Logistics Analysis Program (ILAP). Parts that should be replaced on a scheduled basis (e.g., track) can have their inventory depth limited accordingly.

- – Compute both ROs and ROPs versus just an authorized level. ROs and ROPs are required to operate the Army's supply information system and are needed to ensure proper supply performance. Using appropriate ROs and

---

[12] The EDA has an archive of part orders placed by units on their daily deadline reports or O26 prints that list the units' not-mission-capable equipment. See Eric Peltz et al., *Diagnosing the Army's Equipment Readiness: The Equipment Downtime Analyzer,* Santa Monica, CA: RAND Corporation, MR-1481-A, 2002.

ROPs enhances supply chain efficiency, reduces SSA workload, and ensures that the ASL provides the expected level of service.

- Evaluate the effectiveness of the review and oversight process that leads from automated recommendations to approved requirements. The APS ASLs that did not perform well in OIF did undergo a formal review process that did not catch the problems with the ASLs.

- The Army should establish APS ASLs as turnkey operations so that they can be moved from storage and used immediately.

  - Parts should be stored in an operational configuration within containers with a single storage location for each part. The containers should have storage aids arrayed in a way that provides complete accessibility to SSA personnel as soon as the doors of the containers are opened, with each part in a separate location.

  - The Army should also ensure that all requisite inventory management data are available for seamless data transfer to the field information system, to include ROs, ROPs, and complete location information.

- Ensure that all APS ASLs are used on a periodic basis by operational forces on exercises. This will serve as a twofold check. First, it will enable practice and evaluation of operational startup capabilities to support expeditionary operations. Second, actually using the parts during an exercise and measuring performance will serve as a check on the requirements and funding processes.

Home station (deployable) ASLs

- Embed recent improvements made to the current methodology and piloted for OIF rotations and reset in Army automation. The enhancements incorporate newly available and improved information about which parts drive readiness in the field (i.e., EDA data), precisely targeting parts that are reported on the daily deadline report across the Army rather than relying on essentiality codes and requisition priority.[13]

- Wherever possible, efforts should be made to increase the depth of readiness drivers to account for the higher demand rates and longer replenishment times associated with deployed operations. In particular, for small, inexpensive items depth can often be increased without increasing storage requirements.[14]

---

[13] This has been incorporated in a new methodology termed enhanced dollar cost banding that is currently being used by RAND Arroyo Center to help the AMC expert team develop recommended ASLs for new Army modular organizational designs.

[14] Recent ASL runs made by RAND Arroyo Center have used both OIF and garrison demands along with longer replenishment times. These have been combined with modifications to the economic order quantity formula to increase inventory levels without increasing storage requirements by using available space in bins.

- Centralize the computation of inventory level recommendations under an expert ASL review team within AMC as the first step in the ASL review process. This will allow for more tailoring of input data to precisely reflect task force organization and will support continuous improvement of the ASL methodology, while still leveraging the expertise of local supply managers and maintenance technicians to review the automated output. This should reduce unit workload, as units focus more on the review than on the data preparation and mechanics of generating the initial recommendations for the review process.
  - Develop automation to support rapid ASL computation for deliberately planned task organizations. The automation should enable the use of shorter review periods, the combination of demand streams from different customer units to reflect future support relationships, and the addition of specific end items.
  - In the interim or as a first step, use the recently stood up Army Materiel Command centralized ASL expert team to provide assistance upon request. Until the automation in the previous bullet is developed, the expert team can customize ASL computations to support task organization and the introduction of new end items through database manipulation as is being done for OIF.[15]
- Dynamic battlefield task organization can challenge the efficacy of ASLs produced for units in home station. The Army should analyze options for meeting this challenge. One is to use sub-ASL inventory modules to facilitate dynamic task organization. These might be modules of an ASL that could move with battalions (BNs) or smaller units when they move to another unit. Each module would have to be in a separate container or a modular storage aid within a container that could easily be sent with a unit, which reduces efficiency and increases total storage capacity needed. The module and the remainder of the ASL would have to have separately computed requirements in order for the remainder of the ASL to remain effective upon loss of the module. An alternative model would be to have BN-sized (or other unit sizes) ASL modules available in theater for certain BN types for use when they task organize and become supported by a SSA that does not typically support the type of equipment they have. A third option would be more robust prescribed load lists (PLL) at the company level.[16]

---

[15] RAND Arroyo Center, in conjunction with the ASL expert team, has been developing recommendations for ASLs for units in and deploying to Iraq to support evolving support relationships in the theater.

[16] PLLs are the inventories held at company level. They are typically quite limited in breadth.

ASL performance metrics

- Better align ASL performance metrics to focus only on parts desired for stockage (i.e., readiness drivers, mobility feasible, etc.). Current Army ASL performance metrics consider requests for all items, to include those that are not critical or on ASL-exclusion lists. ASLs should be designed to include only readiness drivers and to exclude items that are not mobility feasible and that can be ordered in large quantities for planned events (e.g., change of track). The metrics should thus indicate how well an ASL is stocking the desired items, not all items, by limiting the population of part requests for accommodation rate and fill rate computation to requests for parts that will have a direct impact on readiness.

Communications connectivity

- Improve the ability to create requests, especially during combat operations. One possibility is to develop user-friendly personal digital assistant (PDA)-like part ordering capabilities for maintenance. Hand-held, point and click, wireless devices that enable real-time part ordering could become part of the future maintenance system.
- Enable always-on, mobile requisition submission capability.[17]

---

[17] This need will be met by the current Army plan to provide all SSAs with mobile satellite communications. See briefing, "Connect the Logistician," HQDA-DALO-SMI, 11 May 2004.

CHAPTER THREE
Theater Distribution

Theater distribution problems in OIF were chronic for supplies other than fuel. The problems were primarily associated with major combat operations and resulted from a lack of adequate transportation capacity stemming from theater setup and other factors. The theater distribution center setup was also considered to be problematic in terms of timing, although negative effects are not clear in the distribution data. Security problems posed major issues for theater distribution in combat operations and then again in 2004 when the insurgency increased in intensity.

Figure 3.1
Key Theater Distribution Characteristics in the Joint Supply Chain Vision (see page 10)

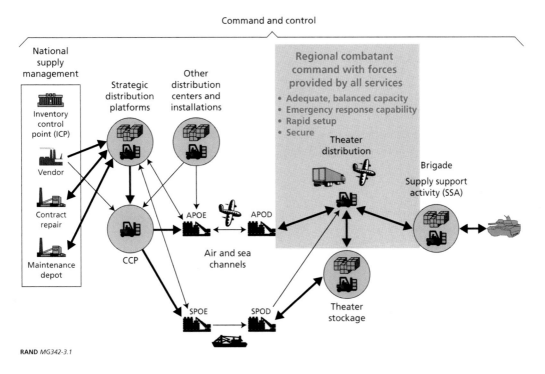

RAND *MG342-3.1*

Insufficient Cargo Truck Capacity During Major Combat Operations

Truck capacity is widely considered to have been below what was needed, and distribution records show evidence of insufficient capacity to move all supplies needed by combat units from the theater distribution center on a daily basis. We found that several reasons led to this situation.

The Planned Cargo Truck Requirement and Availability

We were not able to locate clear documentation of the total cargo truck requirement across echelons. Various organizations developed their own estimates, but we have been unable to document the total theater requirement for the dry cargo distribution system *over time*.[1] The 377th Theater Support Command (TSC) did report a requirement of 930 medium trucks when operations commenced, with just 298 total trucks (including 147 flatbeds and palletized load system (PLS) trucks for dry cargo distribution) on hand including host nation support.[2] The TSC reports that in addition to organic truck shortfalls, host nation and contracted truck support fell short of expectations. This appears to have happened in part because of low operational readiness rates of contract trucks and security issues, with the Iraqi resistance preventing some use of planned contractor truck augmentation. The 3rd Corps Support Command (COSCOM) reported having 20 percent of its requirement at the start of combat operations, with a total of 191 cargo trucks available at the start of combat operations (the 3rd COSCOM reached 1,988 cargo trucks by July 8).[3] Figure 3.2 shows the number of 3rd COSCOM cargo trucks available for use as deployments progressed. Figure 3.3 shows the number of TSC trucks available, and Figure 3.4 shows the combination.

While not a clear benchmark, Operation Desert Storm (ODS) serves as an interesting point of reference. When ground operations started, the approximate ODS ratio was 73 Army personnel per medium truck equivalent, versus about 194 people per medium truck equivalent in OIF.[4] Additionally, in OIF the distance from the

---

[1] Dry cargo includes liquid products in "dry" packages, such as bottled water and cans of oil. The distinction is based upon whether a tanker-type truck is needed.

[2] In an interview, COL Dan Lee, Support Operations Officer, 377th TSC, provided information about the TSC's truck requirement. TSC on-hand truck information is based upon a spreadsheet compiled by the 377th TSC that lists daily truck counts by type and source. It was derived from filled transportation requests from 1 to 25 March and from distributed movement program daily data from 26 March to 30 April 2003.

[3] Interview with BG Charles Fletcher, former commanding general of 3rd COSCOM, 22 October 2003, and 3rd COSCOM weekly truck available spreadsheet archived by 3rd COSCOM Headquarters staff.

[4] Sources: *Theater Logistics in the Gulf War*, Army Materiel Command, 1994; 3rd COSCOM daily commander update briefings; 3rd COSCOM, "Common User Lift Trucks" spreadsheet; OIF Rock Drill, briefing by LTC Dave Powell, RAND Army Fellow, on ODS truck deployments, 1992.

Figure 3.2
3rd COSCOM Common User Cargo Truck Assets

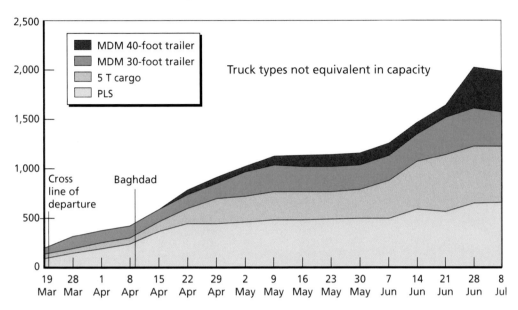

RAND *MG342-3.2*

NOTE: PLS = Palletized Load System truck; 5 T Cargo = 5-ton truck; MDM = medium truck (30 or 40 feet).

Figure 3.3
377th TSC Cargo Trucks

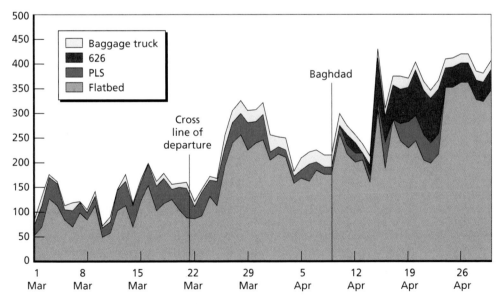

RAND *MG342-3.3*

NOTE: 626 = A truck that has passed a "626" safety inspection to carry bulk ammunition and explosives; Baggage truck = commercial 18-wheel tractor-trailers and their military equivalent M915s.

Figure 3.4
3rd COSCOM and 377th TSC Cargo Trucks

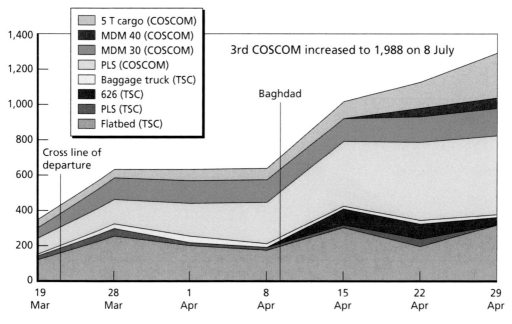

RAND MG342-3.4

NOTE: PLS = Palletized Load System truck; 5 T Cargo = 5-ton truck; MDM = medium truck (30 or 40 feet); Baggage truck = commercial 18-wheel tractor-trailers and their military equivalent M915s.

logistics base to support combat operations was greater—i.e., 285 miles to An Najaf and 344 miles to Baghdad, versus 210 miles from logistics bases to the farthest advance in ODS.[5] As deployments of both trucks and overall forces continued, the ratio improved some by early April 2003, but the support distances increased proportionately to the decrease in the ratio, limiting the effective gain in capacity. Through mid-April this trend continued, with truck counts climbing but doing so along with increases in support distance and the spread of units across Iraq. So in relative terms, the distribution capacity for OIF appears to have been lean.

Deployment Planning
The previous discussion suggests that one reason for insufficient truck capacity was a shortfall against the estimated requirement developed during operational planning. Changes in the deployment plan are widely cited as producing this situation. Widespread interviews relate that units such as truck companies were often treated as indi-

---

[5] In ODS, a logistics infrastructure had been established composed of forward log bases positioned such that the maximum travel distance was about 200 miles one way. Note that in establishing these forward bases, transits on the order of 500 miles one way were needed, but we are focusing on G-Day forward of the line of departure.

vidual elements in the deployment planning process rather than as parts of broader capability packages. Thus, when the need for a unit was questioned, it was difficult to justify in terms of effects on overall combat capabilities. Additionally, a majority of combat service support units are in the reserve component, requiring about 90 to 120 days to mobilize and deploy.[6] So to get ready by the start of combat operations would have required mobilization prior to the December 2002 holiday season. However, in some cases, it was decided to delay the mobilizations until after the holidays. The combined result was that cargo truck units were reportedly deleted or shifted back in the deployment flow through a series of deploying planning conferences and in the request-for-forces process.

This set of deployment planning issues may have been affected by the lack of adequate theater distribution planning tools. No integrating, automated tool enabled comprehensive, consistent planning across echelons. Rather, each echelon used its own tools. For example, the theater support command used spreadsheets and computer-aided design software. Although such methods are effective for deliberate planning, they are less effective for dynamic evaluation as the operational and deployment plans change. This could be important for providing decisionmakers with assessments of how such changes affect sustainability. Additionally, no one had responsibility for looking across the theater and establishing a complete, detailed theater distribution plan and requirements down to the maneuver brigade level. What were in a sense separate plans were not treated as one capability package by the senior echelons of the chain of command. Nor were the separate plans represented by one organization in deployment planning conferences. Additionally, this impedes seamless rebalancing of assets across echelons of distribution when the plan is not executed fully or needs to change because of unexpected conditions.

Unanticipated Demands for Cargo Truck Capacity

Aside from the question of whether the force had sufficient distribution assets to support the plan, two events increased the effective cargo truck requirement:

- A decision to provide support troops with bottled water throughout the operation.
- The unanticipated need to use trucks for unit movements.

Planning assumed that units would cross the line of departure with bottled water, with a transition to bulk water production and five-gallon cans within five days.[7] Subsequently, the decision was made to rely instead on bottled water throughout the operation for a significant portion of hydration needs. This significantly added to

---

[6] Based upon actual times for OIF.

[7] COL James Lee, Support Operations Officer, 377th Theater Support Command, email, 20 July 2004.

cargo distribution demand, with reports of 60 percent of dry cargo "line haul" or lift assets being devoted to bottled water—a need exacerbated by the high bottle break-age rate that occurred when cases of water were broken open or crushed, slowing handling and further increasing demand. In fact, twice as many trucks were used to move bottled water as food.[8]

Another unplanned demand for distribution assets was the use of trucks for unit moves by the 101st Airborne Division (Air Assault) and the 82nd Airborne (ABN) Division's 2nd BCT.[9] One example is having to move the 2nd Brigade of the 82nd ABN (2/82 ABN) to As Samawah. Unexpected resistance and continued threats from *Fedayeen* fighters had tied down the 3/3 ID in the vicinity of As Samawah in part to secure the supply lines. The advance from An Najaf to Baghdad could not continue until the 3/3 ID could join the remainder of the division. The 2/82 ABN relieved the 3/3 ID, requiring the diversion of cargo trucks to help complete the move. Finally, deployment delays and even some planned deployment flows required the use of trucks for force reception in Kuwait.

Factors That Reduced the Effective Capacity of Available Trucks

Distribution capacity depends upon the number of trucks and the daily volume that each truck can move, which depends upon distance, road speed, and utilization. In particular, road speed assumptions and utilization were affected by three factors:

- Road conditions that diverged from expectations.
- Convoy control and road congestion problems.
- The *shamal* or sandstorm.

Expectations about the quality of the main supply route (MSR) that derived primarily from photographic reconnaissance turned out to be wrong. The MSR ap-peared to consist of standard paved, two-lane roads. In reality, the road edges were falling apart, effectively making the route a one-lane road; some stretches turned out to be improved dirt roads. For much of the route, usable shoulders were limited and consisted of talcum powder–type sand. Even these quickly became hard to use be-cause of the dust and the pulverization of the sand. Additionally, the unexpected re-sistance in As Samawah forced all traffic onto an alternative supply route to the west using a bypass that was not paved.[10] The result of these problems was much slower

---

[8] 3rd COSCOM daily commander update briefings.

[9] Email from COL James Lee. Additionally, many descriptions of the operation discuss this need in general terms, although they do not generally cite the fact that this requirement was not planned for and was met through the use of assets intended for sustainment.

[10] Interview with LTG William Wallace, formerly commanding general of V Corps, Fort Leavenworth, Kansas, 6 April 2004; Headquarters, 3rd Infantry Division, Department of the Army, *Operation Iraqi Freedom: Third In-fantry Division (Mechanized) "Rock of the Marne" After Action Report*, Final Draft, 12 May 2003; Fontenot.

movement than the expected 30 kilometers per hour.[11] This increased the requirement for trucks to achieve the desired level of distribution capacity.

Additionally, even though the initial rate of movement was slower than projected and a portion of the MSR was not usable, follow-on units and supplies were not held back in Kuwait. This resulted in heavy congestion on the roads, further slowing traffic. Finally, convoy disruptions resulted in some delays. Some convoys stopped due to enemy action whether direct or in the general vicinity. At other times, drivers stopped when they saw fires or Iraqis under guard,[12] and there are reports of units simply stopping to take an uncoordinated break. There are also reports of drivers, after long periods of continuous operations, falling asleep and blocking traffic, with no one realizing why the convoy had stopped. Having only one driver per truck in some cases contributed to sleep problems as well as the lack of identification of such problems.[13] It should be noted that simply making more trucks available to counter the road speed problem would not have had an effect without improved movement control or the use of additional supply routes as feasible. Similarly, once movement control of trucking is "optimized" and all potential supply routes are used, the force size to be supported via a single line of communication reaches a limit, or alternative modes of distribution must be leveraged.

The second factor that temporarily hindered distribution capacity—in fact, just about shut it off entirely—was the *shamal* or sandstorm. It started in the afternoon of 24 March and ended about midnight on 26 March, with periods during which it became close to impossible to drive. Limited to literally inching along at about two miles per hour with drivers hanging their heads out the sides of vehicles to see the road, some convoys halted entirely.[14] Obviously, more trucks could not have helped during this period. However, a system "on the edge" or even under capacity will have a more difficult time recovering from such a disruption. Inventories that are exhausted during the disruption cannot be quickly replenished to handle further potential disruptions.

Divisional Adaptation to Shortfalls in Cargo Truck Capacity

Once 3rd ID units reached An Najaf and stopped advancing, their organic truck assets became more flexible. The materiel on the trucks, which are in effect mobile warehouses, could be downloaded as necessary in order to send the trucks rearward

---

[11] Interview with MAJ Glenn Baca, formerly Division Transportation Officer, 28 October 2003. CASCOM OIF Rock Drill discussion.

[12] LTC Katherine Cook, email discussion with the author, 2 June 2004.

[13] Interview with BG Charles Fletcher.

[14] Interview with MAJ Pacheco.

to pick up supplies dropped off in the division support area or at corps-level direct support (DS) logistics support areas (LSA). This same approach was feasible even after the advance resumed, as support battalions did not initially cross the Euphrates River and because the advance was no longer continuous and as rapid. Similarly, the limited movement requirements once Baghdad was cordoned provided this flexibility to use organic trucks.

At times this divisional truck asset flexibility became important and probably helps explain why distribution problems could be overcome to a degree. In a sense, organic division and brigade truck assets became an unplanned part of the theater distribution system. COSCOM assets generally did not deliver directly to the BCTs. Rather, supplies were often brought to a central point such as the main support battalion. But the main support battalions themselves (in the 101st ABN and 3rd ID) did not have sufficient transportation assets to deliver to the brigades. So the brigades sometimes had to find ways to go get their supplies.[15] However, the need to download and upload the trucks every time the trucks are used to augment distribution capacity creates additional workload and risk during combat operations and is something the units clearly prefer to not have to do.

Supply Levels During Combat Operations

The 3rd ID's plan was to cross the line of departure with five days of supply of food and water in organizational trucks and trailers, with an additional one to two days of supply in support units, depending upon the unit. Some units within 3rd ID reported up to two additional days beyond the five at the organizational level depending upon how much they could stuff into every nook and cranny of their vehicles (this ease of storage was understood as one advantage of providing troops with bottled water).[16] And some commanders formally directed seven days of supply.[17]

The plan was to get the first resupply two days after commencing operations, with distribution flowing from that point on, keeping the division close to the initial full load of supplies.[18] As a result of the sandstorm, the congested roads, starting the

---

[15] Interview with LTC Willie Williams, formerly commander, 26th FSB, 3rd ID, 22 October 2003.

[16] Interviews at 3rd ID Division Artillery (DIVARTY) with LTC Craig Finley (CDR 1/39 FA BN MLRS), MAJ Phil Rice (Ops, 1/9), MAJ Jim Rooker (Asst S-3), MAJ Benigno (S-3, 1/39), SGT Pichardo, CPT Miguel Garcia (S-4), MAJ Barren (2 BDE Fire Support Officer), MAJ Ken Patterson (current XO), COL Thomas Torrance (CDR) on 28 October 2003. Interviews at 2/3 ID with CPT Jeff Sabatini (A/S-4 Maint and S&S), 1LT Adam Points (Battle Captain), and focus group on 29 October 2003. Interviews at 3-7 CAV with CPT Patrick Shea, 1LT Keith Miller, and CPT David Muhlenkamp on 29 October 2003.

[17] Interview with SGT Pichardo.

[18] Interview with LTC Steve Lyons, formerly commander of 703rd Main Support Battalion, 3rd ID, 28 October 2003.

operation two days early, and the other factors that affected distribution capacity and demand, the first replenishment of food and water, along with limited quantities of other materiel, arrived three days late.[19] At this point, some units were down to a day or less of supplies. Interviews and supply status reports reveal that water was a bigger concern than food.

Early on 26 March, the 19th Support Center's (SC) situation report stated that supplies were en route but delayed by the weather. They expected to see dramatic improvement as the storm lifted and the en route supplies began reaching their destinations. Because of the storm and the other factors discussed, the first push of supplies that left on 23 March did not reach Objective RAMS near An Najaf until 26 March and then had to be distributed to the 3rd ID's BCTs and other units.[20]

The plan was to launch the advance to cordon Baghdad with robust quantities of food, water, and other supplies available in units and at forward LSAs. The original concern was that from this point forward, supply lines would be at high risk, so immediate resupply could not be counted upon. However, many sources combine to indicate that distribution capacity was insufficient to rebuild supplies back to the five-day level. Instead, fairly consistent flow just at or sometimes a little below the ongoing level of consumption was established, generally keeping organizational units sustained at the minimum level to continue operations as planned. The first push of two days worth of food and water did not arrive until 26 March, but another two days of supply was en route for delivery on 27 March with another two days worth scheduled for departure on 27 March for delivery on 29 March.[21] This pattern continued with two-day pushes departing every other day, except for the one on 29 March, which had a four-day push. However, most of the convoys were short some trucks, reducing the convoy loads from the full two days of supply.[22] Additionally, this resupply pattern did not become immediately clear to 3rd ID personnel. With limited visibility of convoys in transit to them (both their location and what they were carrying) at their level, supplies seemed to just show up. This uncertainty dramatically increased the perceived level of risk. Table 3.1 shows the days of supply on hand reported by the 1st BCT of the 3rd ID.

Snapshots of the DS on-hand levels at LSA Bushmaster near An Najaf were archived for a small number of days. They suggest that DS food supply was built up to the target level of two days, but bottled water supplies were thin, often at less than one day of supply.

---

[19] Interview with LTC Steve Lyons.

[20] 19th Support Center SITREP, 261100ZMAR03.

[21] 19th Support Center SITREP, 261100MAR03.

[22] 3rd COSCOM daily commander update briefings, 3 and 5 April 2004.

Table 3.1
Days of Supply on Hand, 1st BCT, 3rd ID Supply Status Reports

	29 March	30 March	31 March	1 April	6 April	7 April	8 April	9 April
MREs	1.6	1.9	1.9	1.8	1.8	1.5	1.5	1.8
Water	0.8	1.0	1.2	1.0	1.0	0.9	0.9	0.8
JP 8 Fuel	1.0	4.3	4.7	3.9	3.1	4.1	3.6	2.3

NOTE: All available daily archives shown.

We do note that the 3rd COSCOM's daily briefings indicate different supply levels of food and water in 3rd ID than indicated by 1/3 ID's supply status reports: 4 to 5 days of supply on 4 and 5 April in the 3rd COSCOM reports for the 3rd ID versus 1 to 2 days reported at the brigade level. This may reflect the amount of materiel at division level and/or en route to BCTs as opposed to the brigade-level view reflected in BCT supply status reports, since corps throughput was to the division support area and not directly to brigades. Table 3.2 includes on-hand days of supply of MREs, bottled water, and bulk water along with bulk fuel and ammunition status and lists of critical Class II, IIIP, and IX supply items as shown in daily 3rd COSCOM briefings.

What the combination of the limited situation reports, commander's update briefings, and brigade supply reports and interviews shows is that the intent was to build supplies in divisional and other major units back up to the original line-of-departure level, with two days of DS backup at LSA Bushmaster. For food it appears this was almost achieved if the supplies in the division support area are combined with the supplies available in BCTs, but limited distribution capability from the DSA forward to units did not make it appear thus to front line maneuver units. Water remained scarcer, even as the daily requirement was reduced from 6 bottles per person to 3 per person after setting up LSA Bushmaster based upon the ability to supplement bottled water with bulk water.[23] The bottom line is that the overall reports reaching corps commander level most likely indicated a stabilizing and sufficient supply situation with respect to the commander's intent to advance forward through the Karbala Gap toward Baghdad, but also that these reports remained interspersed with reports of local shortages. Figure 3.5 shows what the distribution pipeline looked like during combat operations after about 26 March, as constructed from report archives from the various organizations after the fact. This complete view was not available during combat operations.

---

[23] 1st BCT Orange 1 supply status reports, 3rd COSCOM daily commander update briefings.

Table 3.2
Days of Supply on Hand as Reported in 3rd COSCOM Daily Commander Update Briefings

		4 April	5 April	10 April
3rd ID	MRE	4	5	1.8
	Bottled	4	5	1
	Bulk	1	1	1
	IIIB	G	G	G
	V	G	G	G
	Critical	Dextron III	Dextron III	
		Turboshaft	Turboshaft	
		BATT (5590)	BATT (5590)	
82nd	MRE	3	2	3
	Bottled	2	2	1.5
	Bulk	0	0	0
	IIIB	G	G	G
	V	G	G	G
	Critical	Dextron	Dextron	
		Turboshaft	Turboshaft	
			105mm HERA	
			HELLFIREs	
101st	MRE	2.1	3.1	5
	Bottled	5	6	5
	Bulk	0	0	1
	IIIB	G	G	G
	V	G	G	G
	Critical	BATT (5590)	BATT (5590)	

NOTE: G = Green supply status (at the target level/low risk).

Figure 3.5
The MRE, Bottled Water, and Fuel Pipeline During Combat Operations from About 26 March Onward

Estimated days of supply

	BCT	Division LRP/transit	DS/ LSA	Distribution pipeline	GS/ port	"Strategic pipeline"
MRE	1–2	0–2	1–2	2(–)	0–3	Ship
Water	0–1	0–2	0–1	2(–)	4–15	Local supplier/ship
Fuel	3–4		3	Pipeline to Tallil	3+	Refinery and oil field

Capacity Devoted Almost Entirely to Food, Water, and Ammunition

Other items that came through the theater distribution center (TDC) were behind food, water, and ammunition in priority, limiting the frequency with which these items were shipped. Pushes of food and water would come through the TDC, and any available capacity was used to ship spare parts along with Class II, IIIP, and IV materiel. But such capacity was very limited during major combat operations, preventing complete distribution of even critical items that had been identified with spray paint by unit personnel in the TDC yard.[24]

Ammunition Supply During Combat Operations

Ammunition support during combat operations is more problematic in general, because compared to food and water, consumption of ammunition is much more variable and unpredictable and resupply determination is more complex, depending upon the type of ammunition needed. This need is based upon both what has been expended and what types of fights the unit expects to engage in. A term such as "days of supply" has no utility or applicability, as a full load of some ammunition types could be expended in less than an hour or last more than a week, depending upon the situation. Additionally, the need for ammunition resupply can be immediate, without warning, and develop while in contact. Critical, spot shortages requiring immediate, emergency resupply are more likely to develop for ammunition than for other supply classes, and they did; additionally, shortages can develop in difficult resupply situations. But a general, overall shortage did not develop, at least in terms of having some ammunition available to achieve the desired effects, if not by means of the preferred munitions.[25]

3-7 Cavalry's (CAV) intense fight outside of An Najaf on 25 March provides a good example of the challenge of ammunition resupply. With a high rate of fire, 3-7 CAV ran low on small arms as the sandstorm made resupply and external fire support (e.g., close air support) difficult. A 26 March situation report from the 19th SC states that munitions had been loaded aboard CH-47s but were still awaiting a break in the weather before heading out to the 3-7 CAV.[26] The 3-7 CAV had also run low earlier, in fighting around As Samawah. Similarly, 1-64 Armor ran low on small arms in a fight in the vicinity of An Najaf. It remained at green officially but its personnel wanted to top off their supply of ammunition before continuing to Baghdad and were unable to do so because the sandstorm prevented a planned CH-47 resupply. After the sandstorm subsided and the unit was out of immediate danger, the CH-47s

---

[24] Interview with MAJ Thomas Murphree, formerly TDC commander (and previously CFLCC C-4 battle captain), 26 May 2004.

[25] Interview with MG Buford C. Blount, formerly commanding general, 3rd ID (Mechanized), 18 November 2003. Interview with BG Charles Fletcher.

[26] 19th SC Situation Report 26100ZMAR03.

were no longer available for this mission. Eventually, its supporting FSB delivered the ammunition after it was dropped off at Objective RAMS near An Najaf after the advance recommenced.[27]

The 3rd ID took 1.5 days of a unit basic load across the border for large-caliber direct-fire weapons. This represents a turret load in each combat vehicle and half a turret load on trucks. Limiting the amount of ammunition on trucks and at the support battalions enabled the brigades to bulk up on loads of other supplies such as water.[28] From this perspective, it was recognized that some risk had been taken with ammunition, although this seems to be based upon an expectation of limited combat from the border to Baghdad.[29] Multiple units, however, did report shortages of mortar rounds that could potentially have created problems. For example, 1/3 ID reported cases in which it would have liked to use mortars for suppressive fire but did not, in order to conserve rounds for what was believed would be more critical fights south of Baghdad. In consonance with the anticipated need for mortar fire, 1/3 ID used its mortars in a fight east of Baghdad International Airport.[30]

The division artillery (DIVARTY) struggled at times with shortages but invariably found ways to get resupplied. However, the artillery batteries often did not have the types of fuses and munitions that were deemed optimal, and deliveries were made in bulk, requiring the DIVARTY to do break bulk for distribution of combat-configured loads to units. At other times, the only way the DIVARTY could get needed ammunition in a timely manner would be to send division assets to theater ammunition supply points, bypassing the theater distribution system. It is possible that such issues could create problems in some situations. However, the DIVARTY commander and staff reported that there were no cases where they could not achieve the desired combat effects.[31] Still, there were times that shortages produced collateral, undesirable effects, such as when commanders would have preferred to use high-explosive munitions to cut down on duds but had no choice other than to use dual-purpose improved conventional munitions (DPICM) instead of conventional high-explosive shells, because DPCIM was 56 percent of the direct support artillery

---

[27] Interviews with LTC Willie Williams.

[28] Interviews with LTC Steve Lyons and LTC Willie Williams.

[29] Interview with MG Buford C. Blount.

[30] Interviews at 1/3 ID with COL William Grimsley, commander; LTC Ernest Marcone, commander 3-69 AR; and focus group of battalion executive officers, battalion motor officers, battalion S-4s, and maintenance technicians.

[31] Interviews at 3rd ID Division Artillery (DIVARTY) with LTC Craig Finley (CDR 1/39 FA BN MLRS), MAJ Phil Rice (Ops, 1/9), MAJ Jim Rooker (Asst S-3), MAJ Benigno (S-3, 1/39), SGT Pichardo, CPT Miguel Garcia (S-4), MAJ Barren (2 BDE Fire Support Officer), MAJ Ken Patterson (current XO), COL Thomas Torrance (CDR) on 28 October 2003. Interviews at 2/3 ID with CPT Jeff Sabatini (A/S-4 Maint and S&S), 1LT Adam Points (Battle Captain), and focus group on 29 October 2003. Interviews at 3-7 CAV with CPT Patrick Shea, 1LT Keith Miller, and CPT David Muhlenkamp on 29 October 2003.

battalion basic loads provided to the 3rd ID.[32] In particular, DPICM was considered to have an unacceptably high dud rate in softer terrain, such as the sand on the sides of roads,[33] sometimes restricting maneuver and posing threats to military and civilian personnel.[34]

Fuel Supplies Remained Robust

Actions and interviews across all levels lead to the conclusion that the chain of command considered it of paramount importance for the success of the operation to get fuel supply and distribution right. The speed of advance was considered critical to the operational plan, and adequate fuel is essential to a relentless, rapid advance. Unlike some other classes of supply, shortages cannot be temporarily worked around, and fuel cannot be rationed without affecting the operational plan. Perhaps, too, experience from World War II to Desert Storm drove the intense focus on fuel, as it has historically been the most common issue when logistics has constrained mechanized operations.

As a result, a strong emphasis was placed on ensuring that the force would have robust fuel resupply capabilities, which affected the amount of time spent planning and rehearsing fuel resupply operations and the priority given to fuel supply and distribution resources. LTG Wallace stated that "We may have spent more time and energy on fuel at the expense of other commodities in hindsight that we might have anticipated being problems, but we just didn't have the same energy applied to it. . . . We knew we were going to have fuel problems, and thus we spent a lot of time and energy trying to solve those problems . . . and . . . as a result we didn't have any fuel problems."[35]

Theater Preparatory Tasks
Starting in mid-2002, U.S. Central Command and the Coalition Forces Land Component Command (CFLCC) proposed a number of preparatory tasks to set the conditions for sustainment, force reception, and rapid force buildup. The focus was on generating the ability to rapidly receive units and prepare them for combat—essentially developing the infrastructure in Kuwait from airfields to ports to buildings for warehouses and command and control. Most of the approved prepara-

---

[32] Interview with COL Thomas Torrance. "Marne Thunder: 3ID (M) DIVARTY in Operation Iraqi Freedom," briefing, 2003. 3rd ID has recommended changes in unit basic loads, especially for urban operations, with a greater emphasis on high-explosive rounds rather than DPICM.

[33] 3rd ID AAR.

[34] Headquarters, 1st Marine Division, "Operation Iraqi Freedom (OIF) Lessons Learned," 29 May 2003.

[35] Interview with LTG William Wallace.

tory tasks had long lead times, particularly those involving construction.[36] An exception to the construction focus was the early approval to mobilize and deploy seven reserve component fuel truck companies. Five of the seven were alerted on September 14, 2002,[37] and they all arrived between January and March 2003 and were ready when operations commenced. This contrasts with a lack of cargo truck assets and early reserve mobilization in the list of approved preparatory tasks.[38]

The early mobilization and deployment of reserve fuel truck units combined with other preparatory tasks to suggest another focus beyond force reception: developing robust fuel supplies and distribution capabilities. These included the early establishment of fuel "farms"—fuel storage sites—in northern Kuwait and moving the Inland Petroleum Distribution System (IPDS) from Army Prepositioned Stocks (APS) in Qatar to Kuwait by January 2003.[39] Between the IPDS and pipeline construction by the Kuwait National Oil Company, pipelines connected Kuwaiti refineries directly to the fuel farms and led virtually to the border with Iraq, with the fuel infrastructure complete by March 2003.[40] The total system could store 7.3 million gallons of fuel by the start of combat operations, and most storage sites possessed fuel stocks close to capacity.

Besides helping to provide the infrastructure, Kuwait provided the fuel for free, which had two benefits. One was that funds did not have to be approved or allocated from those already available to purchase fuel. Thus funding was not a constraint on building up a fuel stockpile. The other was that the fuel did not have to be transported into Kuwait, which was constrained in its port capacity. Instead it could easily be moved from refinery to the Army's fuel storage farms by pipeline.

Planning and Resourcing Refueling Operations

Maneuver leadership emphasized rigorous fuel planning. Many in the chain of command were thus left with the impression that having enough fuel to get quickly to Baghdad was considered to be the key to initial operations, attributing this to expec-

---

[36] "CFLCC – 1003V Prep Tasks: Setting Theater Support Conditions," 15 February 2003. Tasks: prepositioning of watercraft, improvement of Kuwait Naval Base throughput capabilities, beddown capacity at Kuwait Naval Base, Ash Shuaybah port throughput and staging capacity, Arifjan beddown capacity and base operations, Udairi Airfield construction for rotary-wing beddown, construction for and startup of forward repair activities at Arifjan, establishment of theater stocks for critical items (operational problems delayed use), download of theater war reserve sustainment stocks, aviation depot-level maintenance capability, fuel pipelines and bagfarms, seven fuel truck companies prepositioned, three medium ribbon bridge companies prepositioned, theater ammunition stocks (partial download), and construction and automation for theater support command center at Arifjan.

[37] Office of the Chief of Army Reserve, mobilization tracking spreadsheet.

[38] Interviews with MAJ Thomas Murphree, TDC commander (and previously CFLCC C-4 battle captain), 26 May 2004; "CFLCC – 1003V Prep Tasks" briefing.

[39] Interview with MAJ Thomas Murphree.

[40] In Fontenot (2004).

tations about the enemy and the potential rate of advance. Fuel support was intensively planned and rehearsed across echelons, with requests for fuel assets usually fully resourced. Planning laid out fuel stops down to the hour and even half-hour.[41] By the time operations commenced, confidence in the ability to keep the force fueled was high.[42] In several interviews from battalion to corps commander, leaders looked back and suggested that they should have done the same level of detailed planning for other classes of supply, especially spare parts, testing and rehearsing the process step by step from communications to transportation and receipt.

Generally, fuel distribution assets are acknowledged to have been resourced at requested levels. All echelons received the assets they thought they needed to do the job. Overall, 3rd ID received substantial augmentation of two fuel truck companies, giving the division a total of 170 fuel trucks.[43] To make the maneuver units self-sufficient and allow them to rapidly refuel on the move, these corps assets and MSB fuel truck assets were pushed down to the brigades.[44] For example, 2nd BCT reported a requirement of 60 fuel tankers and in fact had 60 under its control when it crossed the line of departure.[45] As higher echelons had sufficient fuel assets as well, fuel supplies were often brought directly to BCTs, avoiding an intermediate stop and transshipment in the division support area. For dry cargo, in contrast, the limited distribution capacity often forced supplies to be dropped off at a centralized division location, or divisions picked it up from LSAs.[46] Based upon planning, 3rd ID had expected throughput of all supplies to the BCT level,[47] but the lack of cargo assets precluded this from happening.

Additionally, as the force moved forward, large fuel farms were quickly put in place in Iraq and filled, soon representing five days of supply, and these DS supplies continued to be backed up by supplies at fuel farms in Kuwait.[48] Additionally, the

---

[41] Interview with LTC Willie Williams. Interview with MG Buford C. Blount. Interview with COL William Grimsley. 3rd COSCOM movement synchronization briefing.

[42] General discussions and interview with MG Buford C. Blount.

[43] 3rd ID AAR.

[44] LTC Willie Williams, "FSB in Support of Offensive Operations: Personal Notes and After Action Report." Interview with MAJ Glenn Baca.

[45] Interview with LTC Willie Williams.

[46] Interview with COL James Rogers, Commander, Division Support Command, 101st Airborne Division (Air Assault), August 2003. 801st Main Support Battalion AAR; and the 101st Airborne Division (Air Assault) Memorandum for Record, Subject: Operation Iraqi Freedom AAR, 19 May 2003. Interviews at 3rd ID Division Support Command with LTC Bobby Towery (3rd FSB CDR), LTC Michael Armstead (26th FSB CDR), LTC Nate Glover (formerly 603rd ASB XO, then DISCOM S-3), LTC Suzanne Hickey (DMMC Chief), LTC Bill Gillespie (DMMC Chief), MAJ Mark Weinerth (26th FSB SPO), LTC Jack Haley (703rd MSB CDR), and COL Brian Layer (DISCOM CDR) on 29 October 2003.

[47] Interviews with 3rd ID DISCOM.

[48] 3rd COSCOM daily commander update briefing, 8 April.

maneuver forces generally maintained fairly healthy levels. For example, from 29 March to 9 April, 1/3 ID supply status reports showed more than three days on hand on most days.[49]

Differences Between the Fuel and Other Supply Chains

However, beyond the recognized importance of getting the supply and distribution of fuel right, there are other factors unique to fuel supply and distribution that were important as well. Table 3.3 compares how these factors affected fuel supply and distribution performance to how they affected dry cargo supply and distribution performance. The shaded rows are the factors for which a difference was seen.

A frequently cited factor for fuel success is that there was effectively a single fuel supply and distribution owner, the commander of the 49th Quartermaster Group (Petroleum and Water).[50] He could coordinate and balance assets from Kuwait to Baghdad.

Another important factor is that there are no issues related to determining what fuel to send forward, deciding how to package it, and ensuring that the right fuel gets to the right unit. The more complex and variable the demands for a given supply class are, the more critical these decisions become, affecting the load configuration

Table 3.3
A Comparison Between Fuel and Dry Cargo Supply and Distribution in OIF

Factor	Fuel	Dry Cargo
Requirement	Met	Not met
Division and brigade augmentation	Yes	No
Detailed planning	Yes	Less
Early deployment	Yes	No
Cost/financial risk	Free/none	Funding required
Load configuration	Single item	Critical for some classes
Demand: plan and policy changes	Below expectations	Above expectations (e.g., water)
DS inventory points	Large	Limited
Theater distribution system owner	Yes	No
Movement rates (road conditions)	Slow	Slow
Weather	Delay from *shamal*	Delay from *shamal*
In-transit visibility/ situational awareness	Limited	Limited

[49] 1/3 ID Orange 1 supply status reports.

[50] In Fontenot (2004); OIF Distribution Rock Drill After Action Review held at Fort Lee, Virginia (discussion notes).

Table 3.4
Criticality of Load Configuration/Ability to Push Supplies Depends Upon Supply Class Complexity and Demand Variability

Class of Supply	Number of Unique Items
IIIB, bulk fuel	1 (JP-8) for vehicles plus limited amounts of motor gasoline
Water	1 (bulk and bottled)
MREs	1
Unitized group rations (UGR)	4
IV, construction materiel	40 (combat maneuver brigade)
IIIP, packaged POL	81 (combat maneuver brigade)
V, ammunition	112 (combat maneuver brigade)
II, tools, general supplies, clothing, personal gear	1,155 (combat maneuver brigade)
IX, spare parts	10,000 (combat maneuver brigade during combat operations)

SOURCE: 1/3 ID Orange 1 supply status reports and Corps Theater Automatic Data Processing Service Center (CTASC) document history files.

process and whether supplies can be pushed or must be shipped upon demand. Table 3.4 illustrates how supply class complexity varies, and there was a high correlation between class complexity and supply and distribution effectiveness in OIF. There is great benefit to a single fuel type on most of the battlefield.

Another factor is that the demand for fuel was lower than expected. This contrasts greatly to dry cargo, which experienced higher-than-expected demand, especially due to the extended use of bottled water as well to satisfy unit move requirements.

The Pause in the Advance at Objective RAMS

Various reasons have been offered for the well-known "pause" that occurred a few days after the advance began, including supply shortages in V Corps. Thus, we examined whether sustainment problems did indeed generate the pause.

By 23 March, the 2nd BCT of the 3rd ID had secured Objective RAMS just south of An Najaf, and the 1st BCT moved north of RAMS to Objective RAIDERS. However, the 3rd BCT had to counter the unexpectedly heavy resistance in As Samawah that had been interdicting the main supply route and then remained there to protect the LOCs. Then on 24 March the "Mother of All Storms" began, limiting offensive and other operations through the 26th. During this time, the 1st BCT, 2nd BCT, and 3-7 CAV were engaged with enemy forces in the vicinity of An Najaf, which, it was realized, could not be bypassed without incurring undue supply line risk. Similarly, the continued, unexpected resistance by *Fedayeen* along the supply lines led to a change in plans. The route from Kuwait to An Najaf could not be left unprotected. However, with the rolling start to the operation that limited available forces when operations commenced, no combat forces had been following the 3rd ID to secure the rear areas; this was a risk that had been accepted but in anticipation of different reactions from Iraqis to the advance of U.S forces. Thus, the 3/3 ID stayed back to secure critical areas near As Samawah. Plans had to be quickly developed for its relief to enable the 3rd ID to be at full strength for the assault toward Baghdad. Similarly, the *Fedayeen* operating from An Najaf posed too much of a threat for the 3rd ID to continue its advance without another force securing LSA Bushmaster and the supply lines in this area.

Plans were modified to relieve the 3rd ID as soon as possible given the available forces. The 2nd BCT of the 82nd Airborne Division was released to V Corps on 26 March, and it completed its relief of 3/3 ID on the 29th. Plans for the 101st Airborne Division (Air Assault) were changed and it too was assigned to relieve the 3rd ID of LOC security roles. Responsibility for eliminating the threat from irregular forces in An Najaf was also given to the 101st, which completed its move to An Najaf by 30 March.[51] This series of actions enabled the 3rd BCT to move north, rejoining the 1st and 2nd BCTs and allowing the entire division to prepare to restart the offensive before first light on 31 March. During this time, airpower worked to attrit the Medina Republican Guard division and other forces south of Baghdad, setting the conditions for the advance.[52]

Because of the limited distribution capacity and competing demands for the assets, the COSCOM was not able to establish significant stockpiles at LSA Bushmaster. However, the pause in the advance still may have helped the logistics system become somewhat better prepared for further offensive operations. It most likely enabled the distribution system to stabilize after the initial advance and kept the supply lines and thus round-trip times from getting even longer. Every day until the advance resumed was another day for trucks to become available for use as units continued to download their equipment from ships and prepare for operations at camps in Kuwait. From 19 March to 1 April, the 3rd COSCOM's available trucks increased by 63 percent. So while the units and LSA Bushmaster did not fully achieve the desired level of days of supply for food and water, the pipeline from Kuwait north began to approach the desired levels of supply and could maintain a large-enough volume of distribution flow by this time to keep up with consumption (but not enough to build stockpiles or replenish initial unit inventory levels).

---

[51] In Fontenot (2004).

[52] 3rd Infantry Division AAR.

The pause was not caused by a wait to build up stockpiles, although it may have helped the distribution system to stabilize and improve its organization. However, one of the key proximate causes was the need to secure the supply lines to enable continued sustainment and even more extended LOCs. In this sense, beyond any shortfalls in combat service support units themselves, sustaining the force required much greater resources than anticipated: an entire division plus to secure the supply lines from Kuwait through An Najaf.

Additionally, this was certainly not a pause in combat, as should be clear from the descriptions of the operation from 24 to 27 March. The words of LTG McKiernan, the CFLCC commanding general, are stronger. He said, "I would refute any notion that there was any kind of operational pause in this campaign. There was never a day, there was never a moment where there was not continuous pressure put on the regime of Saddam."[53] The protection of the LOCs marked a shift in nature of the operation and in the understanding of the enemy. Rather than the anticipated battles with capable Iraqi armored divisions, the Army had to contend with irregular forces throughout much of the country.

While supply line security remained a concern through the operation, the subject came into play as a major issue from April 2004 through the writing of this report. As the insurgency grew in strength, some supply routes had to be temporarily cut off until they could be resecured.

Recommendations

- Develop improved, integrated theater distribution planning tools. Effective, easy-to-use automation should be made available to help plan and adapt the complete theater distribution system. The tools should be able to rapidly calculate the likely effects of changes to the operational plan and support policies, and should automatically address the implications of battlefield uncertainty in terms of recommended "reserve" requirements. Significant strides appear to have been made toward this vision, with the Joint Deployment Logistics Model (JDLM) used in conjunction with the Integrated Logistics Analysis Program (ILAP) and in-transit visibility data to form the Logistics Common Operational Picture (LCOP) in OIF, and they appear to be continuing with the development of the Battle Command Sustainment Support System (BCS3), which will incorporate JDLM/LCOP functionality.[54] It is imperative that this effort stay

---

[53] In McKiernan, 23 April 2003.

[54] "Operational Requirements Document for the Battle Command Sustainment Support System (BCS3) (Combat Service Support Control System (CSSCS))," Change Number 3.7, 5 November 2003. Army RDT&E Budget

on track and that the final product support deliberate planning, crisis action planning, and decisionmaking to the highest levels by better explaining the rationale for resource requests and the implications of potential decision directions.

- Develop integrated, modular theater sustainment capabilities. The capabilities to be provided should be the starting point for a deployment plan and the development of force packages. Then the units needed to provide these capabilities can be easily linked to the broader capability they serve. The result should be a clear mapping of unit types to capabilities to mission needs, making deployment planning and changes more effective and efficient. In the deliberate force planning process, the Army should ensure that unit building blocks are the right size to enable seamless, phased buildup of capabilities.[55]

- At a minimum, plan and, to the extent possible, set up distribution systems in exercises from brigade to theater level. Either new exercises focused on the development of theater sustainment systems should be developed, or current exercises should incorporate this requirement and logistics setups that better reflect real-world conditions should be incorporated in exercises such as at the National Training Center.

- Address water supply and distribution policies to ensure that planning and execution are aligned. The crucial issue is to ensure that the policy planned for a contingency is the one executed. A high-level policy on whether bottled water will be the preferred option for operations (particularly early operations) should be made by the Army's requirements community in coordination with regional combatant commands, and then plans should be built in accordance with that policy. As issues with water taste and battlefield distribution are addressed, this policy should be revisited.

- DoD should designate a theater distribution system integrator or owner within a regional combatant command.[56] One organization and leader should know the details of the entire theater supply and distribution plan in order to ably communicate the requirements as an integrated whole in the contingency operational and deployment planning processes. Additionally, this organization should work to examine points at which the various portions of the system are

---

Justification (R2 Exhibit), Combat Service Support Control System (Project 091), February 2004. COL Tim Kleppinger, "LCOP Logistics Common Operating Picture Key to BCS3," briefing, February 2004.

[55] The Army has generated significant momentum toward creating these types of capabilities as a result of the work being done under the rubric of modular force development and the G-4's focus area on improving force reception. See Deputy Chief of Staff, G-4, Headquarters, Department of the Army, "Improve Force Reception," Army Logistics White Paper, October 2004.

[56] Developing the ability to "provide unity of effort" within theater distribution is one of the key objectives set forth in Deputy Chief of Staff, G-4, Headquarters, Department of the Army, "Modernize Theater Distribution," Army Logistics White Paper, October 2004.

not integrated, which will often occur if one organization has incorrect assumptions about the resources and practices of either its suppliers or its customers. Once operations begin, the role will shift to integrated execution management and continual examination of the need for changes in the overall scheme of distribution.

CHAPTER FOUR

Strategic Distribution

By strategic distribution we mean the network of activities charged with storing, packing, consolidating, and transporting military materiel from CONUS or other locations outside of the area of operations to Army units in OIF. Strategic transportation has been able to maintain a fairly consistent, scheduled flow of transportation to the theater, albeit with some periods of perturbation, but problems with packing and consolidating materiel prevented fast end-to-end distribution all of the way to the ordering unit. Generally, the system had the ability to rapidly adjust and shift airlift

Figure 4.1
Key Strategic Distribution Characteristics in the Joint Supply Chain Vision (see pages 10–11)

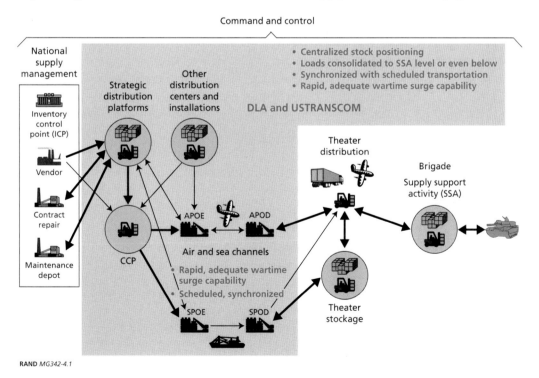

RAND MG342-4.1

capacity to changing demands through the use of commercial air charters and the management of military aircraft prioritization. However, significant problems developed in the warehouse operations and load-building portions of the strategic distribution system, leading to both CONUS delays and downstream effects in theater.

Air Shipment Performance

Shipments from CONUS sent directly for units in theater that were dispatched via strategic air tended to take much longer than expected until the beginning of 2004. Moreover, especially from March to June 2003, problems with the consolidation of shipments led to a high rate of shipments delivered to the wrong units. Many of these shipments were kept and consumed by the receiving unit rather than redirected to the requesting unit. Lateral redistribution among units and returns remained a relatively low priority, given the tremendous workload faced by units and the general shortages that made most items valuable to whatever unit received them.

Figure 4.2 displays average requisition wait time (RWT) in days for shipments sent by air to the theater. The top series shows RWT for items sent on pallets constructed at aerial ports of embarkation (APOE) by Air Mobility Command, and the bottom series shows RWT for items shipped in consolidation and containerization point (CCP)-built pallets. The latter has accounted for 93 percent of shipments sent by air through the course of OIF but only about 60 percent of the weight, as many of the large, heavy items are sent straight to the APOEs for shipment.[1] The first two data points for each series show performance to Kuwait in calendar years 2001 and 2002 to serve as a theater baseline (albeit one that is not completely fair as a point of comparison, since it does not account for the extended theater distribution system now in place for units in Iraq). The remaining data points show monthly times from January 2003 to November 2004. From 9 or 10 days to Kuwait prior to OIF, times climbed to as high as 33 days on average in September for shipments in CCP pallets before beginning to recover. Materiel on APOE pallets has continually taken longer. Lacking the effective synchronization of CCP pallet flow, before OIF these deliveries took twice as long as CCP pallet shipments. Note, however, that for a period in mid-2003, the two modes of air shipments converged with regard to RWT. As we will see, this is due in large part to how CCP pallets were built. Problems with load consolidation largely eliminated the CCP-pallet advantage until they were resolved in

---

[1] For pallets built at the CCP, the distribution channel is termed MILALOC or Military Air Line of Communication. MILALOC accounted for only 40 percent of the air shipping weight through July 2003. Since September 2003, over 70 percent of air shipments in terms of weight have gone MILALOC as DLA started building pallets at its Red River, Texas distribution center, which provides many big, heavy items such as track.

Figure 4.2
RWT for Strategic Air Shipments to Army Units in OIF, Without Backorder Time

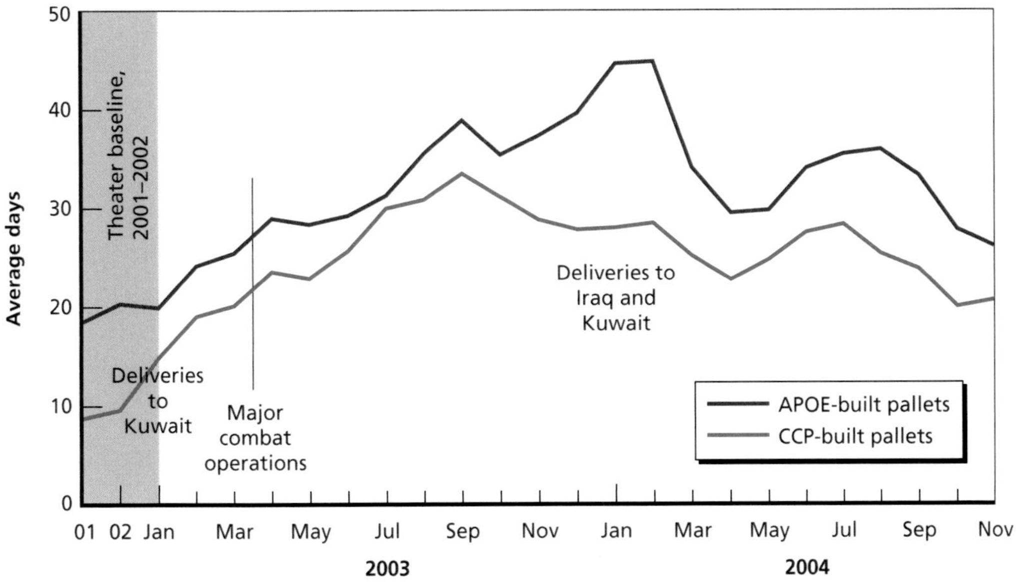

RAND MG342-4.2

November 2003, and the two lines begin to diverge again at that point. In March 2004, CFLCC worked out a new pallet-build policy with Air Mobility Command, leading to improved alignment of load consolidation at APOEs with the theater distribution setup and capabilities. Immediately, dramatic improvement is seen in RWT for shipments delivered via APOE-built pallets. The lower volume of materiel sent to the ports and some special requirements, such as for hazardous materiel, prevent complete replication of CCP practices at the APOE, but some degree of convergence is seen in the data as the two flows once again became much more similar, this time in the right direction.

In some respects, the picture in Figure 4.2 is deceptive or at least incomplete. A new metric became important in OIF, the percentage of shipments reaching the actual requestor and being receipted. Many shipments were sent to the wrong unit and not redirected to the ordering unit, especially from March to June 2003. Figure 4.3 shows these percentages for OIF overall with the same APOE and CCP pallet split. One sees that the problem has continued for APOE-built pallets for most of OIF, driven by how the loads have been consolidated on these pallets. A third series shows the rate for 3rd ID shipments, which dipped to only 50 percent once combat began. The brief downturn in February 2004 is associated with redeployments and deployments for OIF 2, the rotation of forces in early 2004, reflecting a system that continues to have transition problems in its processes.

Figure 4.3
Strategic Air Shipment Receipt Rate in OIF

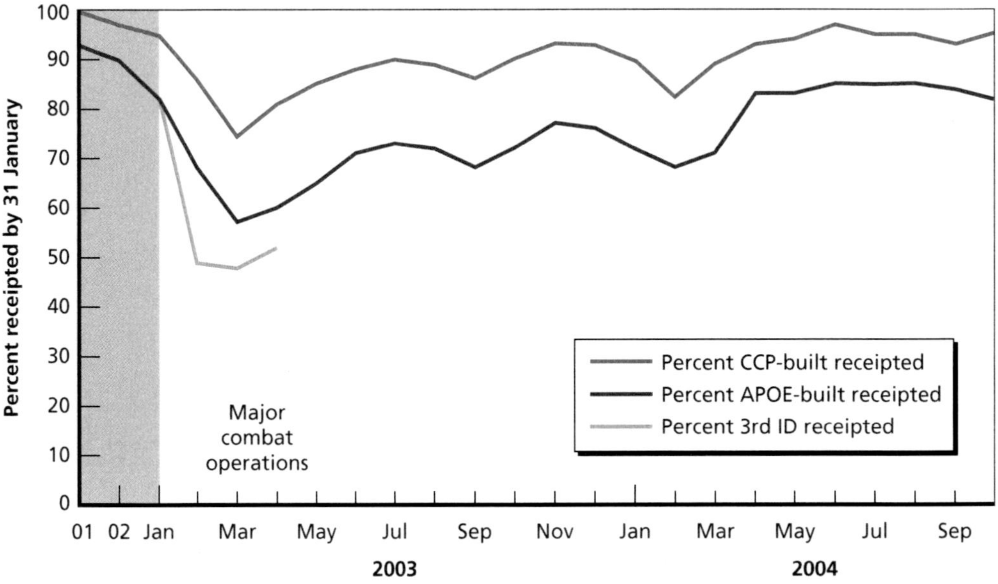

The Sources of Delays for CCP-Built Pallets

To diagnose the sources of problems in the distribution system, a broad set of diagnostic metrics is needed, to include the process segment times shown in Figure 4.4. Segments either reflect the time within a distribution node, waiting or being processed, or the time it takes to get from one node to another. Each set of columns in the chart reflects the average time for a process segment, first for calendar years 2001 and 2002 and then for each month from January 2003 to November 2004.

- The first segment (**order**) reflects a set of information processes for transmitting the order to the national supply system and reflects the time from the document date until the order is received and established in the national supply system.
- The next segment (**source**) is the time for the organization that manages the part to send a materiel release order to a distribution center or other supply organization, which can be either an automated or manual process.
- **Warehouse operations** consist of the set of processes to get an item from storage and prepare it for shipment, and they end when the item departs the warehouse or is released to the shipper.

Figure 4.4
MILALOC Receipt Rates and Process Segment Times, CY01, CY02, and January 2003 to November 2004

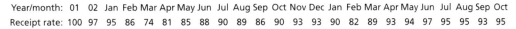

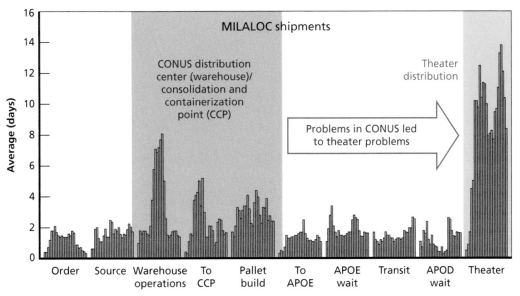

RAND MG342-4.4

- **To CCP** is the time it takes to go from the warehouse to the CCP, ending when it is receipted at the CCP. Time in this segment can come from transportation from a non-collocated distribution center or sitting in a queue waiting for CCP receipt.
- **Pallet build** is the time from when an individual shipment is receipted at the CCP until it is put on the pallet and the pallet is released for shipment.
- **To APOE** reflects the time from CCP release until APOE receipt and includes transportation to the APOE and wait time on both ends.
- Once the APOE receipts the pallets, the wait time for aircraft departure is recorded in the **APOE wait** time segment.
- **Transit** reflects overseas shipment, including intermediate stops and any change of planes.
- **APOD wait** time is how long it takes to leave the APOD once it hits the final aerial port.
- The final segment (**theater**) is the total time from APOD release to receipt by the requestor.

While there are opportunities for improvement in other segments as well, Figure 4.4 draws attention to the set of processes that occur in CONUS distribution centers, to include CCPs, and theater distribution. It shows the mean time for the baseline years and by month for OIF, as well as the receipt rates on the top of the figure. The three distribution center processes went from a sum of 3 to 3.5 days to a maximum total of 15.5 days, and monthly theater distribution time peaked at 12.5 days with a monthly best of 4.4 days (April 2004) since shipments started going into Iraq. In the remainder of this chapter, we will discuss how problems with how loads were built at the CCP (and at APOEs) contributed to problems in theater distribution and what caused the delays in CONUS distribution center/CCP operations.

Load Consolidation

Most small items for Army units shipped from DLA distribution centers, the primary source from which "on-demand" and ASL replenishment orders are filled, are combined in boxes typically addressed to one SSA, as per the supply chain model. That is, all of the orders for a given SSA and its supported units are combined in one or more large boxes, which are called multipacks. These boxes typically contain dozens if not over a hundred shipments. This is the standard practice for DLA.

For shipments to most overseas locations, most of these multipack boxes, containing materiel from the various DLA distribution centers, GSA warehouses, lateral shipments from other Army locations, and direct vendor delivery items, are further consolidated on pallets for air shipment (or in containers for ocean shipment), along with loose, often bigger and heavier items.[2] Prior to OIF, most divisional SSAs and some nondivisional SSAs received air pallets built exclusively for them—one SSA per pallet, again in accordance with the ideal supply chain model.

When pallet loads have materiel for one SSA only, they can go from the CCP in CONUS to the SSA without stopping for resorting and repackaging. However, in OIF and primarily early on, many multipacks contained materiel for multiple SSAs. Some multipacks were used simply to consolidate small loose shipments for transportation; such multipacks were sent to the TDC. This occurred when DLA did not know which SSA the materiel should be sent to. CCP pallets remained mixed through November 2003, and APOE pallets were mixed into early March 2004.[3]

---

[2] In CONUS, scheduled trucks are packed by SSA to enable a "milk run" that drops off materiel at each of the SSAs on an installation.

[3] The basic process for both led to pallets that were mixed, but mixed across SSAs differently, as described later. However, some pallets had only single SSAs, which occurred by chance or as the result of some order characteristics (e.g., a large, single order of tires sufficient to fill an entire pallet). Some APOE pallets for low-volume SSAs will continue to be mixed beyond March 2004, but this will represent a very small percentage of the pallets sent to the theater.

Figure 4.5 illustrates the ideal configurations for multipacks and pallets and examples of what "bad" configurations looked like in OIF. Photographs of multipacks and pallets are provided as well.

Mixed Multipacks

To build multipacks, DLA's distribution centers employ what is termed sortation logic. Each designated SSA gets a separate multipack build location at the bottom of a chute, and packages for delivery to the SSA, whether just passing through to a supported unit or for the ASL, are automatically sent there. So as the foundation of the sortation logic, DLA has to maintain a current list of SSAs to receive shipments, with updates to the list flowing quickly from the Army. DLA also has to have a way of knowing which SSA multipack box a shipment goes in when the order comes directly from a supported unit rather than a SSA.

Figure 4.5
Box (Multipack) and Pallet Configurations

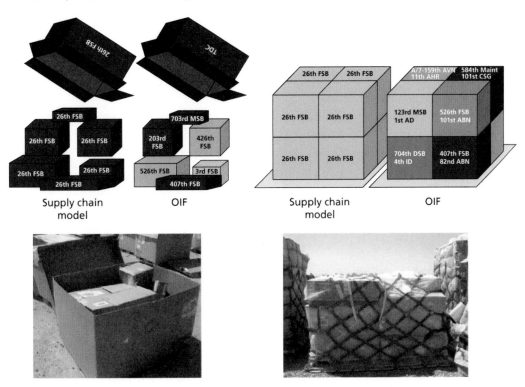

Before OIF, all of the SSAs were appropriately set up to have chutes and receive "SSA-pure" or single-SSA multipacks.[4] Each SSA is recognized by a Department of Defense Activity Address Code (DODAAC), which every unit also has. So in effect, DLA had chutes for specified SSA DODAACs and knew how to map unit DODAACs to SSA DODAACs.

The start of the problem in OIF was the Army's decision to use so-called "sterile DODAACs." To cleanly track and separate OIF expenditures from non-OIF expenditures, every unit and SSA received a new DODAAC for OIF. With better Army and DLA processes for communicating information from the Army and for changing the sortation logic, distribution problems associated with the use of sterile DODAACs probably could have been overcome. But given the processes in use at the time for maintaining the sortation logic—a process that few if any in the Army understood at a detailed level—their introduction contributed significantly to problems in maintaining the quality of the logic and thus to distribution problems. The Army's sterile DODAAC decision required that DLA reconfigure its packing and consolidating activities to align with a new list of SSA and unit DODAACs to a much greater degree than it would have had to do if home station DODAACs had been used. For the SSAs that deployed, their chutes were tied to home station DODAACs, not their new ones, and their supported units were no longer mapped to them. When sterile DODAACs were first "turned on," DLA did not recognize the new SSA DODAACs as multipack or "ship-to" locations, did not know which new DODAACs were SSAs, and did not know which supported unit DODAACs mapped to the new SSA DODAACs.

Getting the updated SSA DODAAC information to DLA and keeping it updated in a timely manner proved to be difficult, particularly over the first few months of OIF. The list of deployed SSA and unit DODAACs and their relationships were provided by U.S. Army Central Command (ARCENT) and CFLCC to DLA via spreadsheet. DLA was not given advance warning of when new SSA DODAACs would be turned on, nor was the spreadsheet updated and resent every single time a new SSA DODAAC was set up. Additionally, there were sometimes delays in getting an updated spreadsheet to DLA. Once it received the spreadsheet, DLA had to manually enter the information—sometimes thousands of DODAACs, with profiles for each DODAAC entered through a series of screens, essentially establishing a lookup table that mapped unit DODAACs to SSA DODAACs for shipment consolidation. Entry was not prioritized by DLA to the several dozen SSAs first. Nor was such prioritization indicated on the spreadsheet by the Army.

In fact, just entering the new DODAACs for just the deploying SSAs would have assured that most shipments reached most units in OIF without error. This is

----

[4] Sometimes multiple SSAs share a single chute, with boxes for each of the SSAs at the bottom. DLA employees use bar code readers to ensure that they put items in the correct box in such situations.

because the standard Army practice is for supported unit requests to come into the SSA and then be converted into a requisition from the SSA itself.[5] When this practice is followed, requisitions have the SSA DODAAC in the document number. For OIF 1, the initial set of deployments for OIF, all major units followed this practice except for the 4th ID, which employed what are called dedicated requests that pass directly through the SSA to the national system when the requested item is not available at the SSA. Thus, these requests maintain the ordering unit's DODAAC in the document number. However, it is still possible for DLA to map these requests to SSAs for shipment even without the entry of the complete customer DODAAC to SSA DODAAC set of relationships, because the dedicated requests also have the SSA DODAAC embedded in the request information in another data field called the supplementary address. Another field in the request, termed the signal code, tells DLA whether the shipment should be sent to the ordering DODAAC or to the DODAAC in the supplementary address. In standard Army practice, the signal code for dedicated requests is used to ensure that they are sent to the SSA, which then distributes shipments to its supported units.[6] Thus, the primary problem driving mixed multipacks for OIF 1 was not having the new sterile SSA DODAACs immediately entered in DLA's Distribution Support System (DSS) as ship-to destinations. If the SSA DODAAC is not recognized within DSS, then even if RON/DON (see footnote 5) is used or a dedicated request has the correct signal code, a distribution center will not know which SSA to send a shipment to.

A combination of factors led to the mixed multipack problem: DLA's lack of understanding of the Army theater distribution and unit structure that resulted in inefficient entry of information in the DLA sortation automation, a sometimes delayed flow of information from the Army component command to DLA, a lack of information flow prioritization consistent with its distribution structure by the Army, a labor-intensive set of processes, and, in OIF 2, incorrect signal codes on some Army requests. One can see that a complex system has evolved for determining what shipments should go into what multipacks. As with most complex systems, this presents many opportunities for error. OIF strained this system to the breaking point because of large-scale and often rapid changes of DODAACs and support relationships.

---

[5] This is a practice termed RON/DON, which represents the establishment of a due-out at the SSA to fill a customer Request Order Number (RON) and the submission of a Document Order Number (DON) to the national supply system. This allows the SSA to consolidate RONs for the same part, fill RONs in order of priority, and to automatically satisfy RONs when a replenishment order for the part arrives before the RON's "associated" DON.

[6] However, there were times when Army organizations applied the incorrect signal code, which is a problem that appears to be correctable through changes in procedures or through changes in automation. In this case, though, DLA would see a unit DODAAC that it did not recognize as a ship-to destination (such a unit would not have a valid shipping address) and revert to its lookup table, which would take care of the problem as long as the lookup table was up to date. There are also some exceptions in which the Army directs the shipment directly to a unit, bypassing the SSA, such as when an Army National Guard unit's home station is not close to its supporting SSA.

Figure 4.6 displays the results of this process. It shows the percentage of shipments in SSA-pure multipacks. When most units first deployed, their SSAs often did not get their own multipacks for the first several weeks. Rather, their materiel ended up in multipacks addressed to the TDC or even in multipacks for other SSAs. The latter case was particularly problematic, as the TDC would have no way to know that the multipack was mixed and would thus send it on to the SSA it was addressed to. Thus, the shipments inside the box for other SSAs would be misshipped, and redistribution of such misshipments to the correct SSA was haphazard. As the tables were updated, sent to DLA, and entered into DSS, the newly deployed SSAs would begin to get their own multipacks.

Mixed Pallets

The DODAAC information is critical for SSA-pure pallets as well, but the causes of mixed SSA pallets go beyond the information flow and sortation logic change problems. In the 1990s, the Army and DLA had worked hard to institute service directly to every major SSA. In CONUS this meant the initiation of scheduled trucks, with the trucks loaded in SSA order so that they could do a "milk run" (a multiple-stop delivery route like those once typified by milk deliveries) around each installation, stopping at each SSA and quickly dropping off its materiel. For OCONUS this

Figure 4.6
Percentage of SSA-Pure Multipacks from January Through October 2003

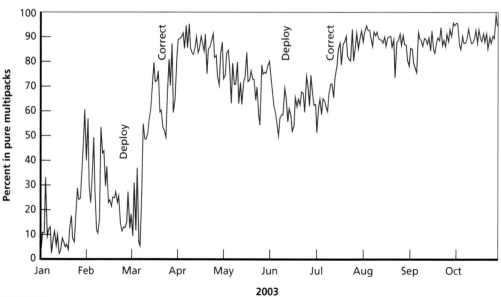

meant SSA-pure pallets that could be delivered through a synchronized theater distribution network that took the pallets from the APOD to SSA without delays for repackaging. Thus, prior to OIF, most SSAs in U.S. Army Europe (USAREUR) and Eighth U.S. Army in Korea received SSA-pure pallets. This included 1st Armored Division (AD) and some 3rd COSCOM SSAs that deployed from Europe to Iraq.

While this had been a standard practice and reflected *Army* doctrine, in post-OIF review it is clear that it had not yet become embedded in *joint* policy, and processes had not been developed to rapidly handle changes in the list of SSAs requiring pure pallets. Even so, the practice was fairly ingrained, so ARCENT/CFLCC planners assumed that it would continue. They requested it from DLA during planning conferences, at least as early as September 2002. It was their impression that this was given the go-ahead, although no formal request and approval took place—nor did they think this would be necessary.

As the volume of shipments started ramping up in early 2003 and more than a couple of SSAs deployed, it soon became apparent that shipments were not consolidated by SSA. In part this was due to the lack of good SSA DODAAC flow from ARCENT/CFLCC to DLA. But it was also due to lack of an agreed-upon plan to do so. Materiel was arriving on pallets mixed across divisions and other major units. As with mixed multipacks, the fact that they were mixed in this way was not always clear, and so the full mixed pallet might be sent to a single SSA, leading to misshipments. In response to the situation, CFLCC formalized the requirement in a message on 2 March 2003, which asked for SSA-pure pallets with a backup plan for broader consolidation to division level, for example, when volumes were too low for SSA-pure pallets. It appears that due to miscommunication and a lack of DLA understanding of Army terms, structure, and unit composition and capabilities, DLA implemented the backup plan as the primary option in mid-March 2003. This plan consolidated loads by geographic region, such as a division and its collocated corps support group (CSG). Shipments would then be sent to a designated lead SSA, often a main support battalion, which would have to break, sort, repack, and distribute the materiel. These units were not designed and thus not manned and equipped to do so, which significantly contributed to the development of backlogs at some of the lead SSAs.

The miscommunication and misunderstandings continued until November 2003, when sufficient information and proof had been provided to all parties clarifying what was really happening and what effects it was having on theater distribution. At that point, CFLCC reemphasized the need for pure pallets, and DLA quickly implemented a SSA-pure policy at the CCP. A critical part of the resolution to the problem was having the right diagnostic metrics to clarify practices and demonstrate the benefits and problems associated with different practices.

Aerial Port Pallets

Aerial ports were a different matter. Some materiel, by rule, gets sent to APOEs for shipment consolidation rather than going through the CCP. Materiel that bypasses the CCP includes hazardous, oversized, sensitive, and other specially designated items. However, aerial ports were never set up as distribution center/CCP–type operations. They just built pallets to support efficient transportation, consolidating pallets by APOD, regardless of unit or service. This is how APOE support (APOE pallet building) to OIF started.

When ARCENT/CFLCC worked with DLA to get CCP SSA-pure pallets, resulting in the geographic region pallets instead, they also got a commitment from Air Mobility Command to build service-pure pallets at Charleston Air Force Base, the main CONUS APOE for forces in OIF. In the end, this does not seem to have helped much, as Army pallets often had materiel for units in different divisions in completely different parts of Iraq.

A problem arose in that these pallets did not appear markedly different from CCP pallets, and not everyone in CFLCC knew the precise CCP and APOE practices. The result was that for an extended period, many of these pallets were sent straight to a single division without first being broken down, even though they contained materiel for multiple divisions or nondivisional units. This produced the much lower receipt rate for APOE-built pallets than for CCP-built pallets. One can also see, though, that until November 2003, nearly all pallets were mixed, so most had to be broken down somewhere in theater, whether they were built at a CCP or an APOE. Thus, RWT for shipments sent via CCP-built and APOE-built pallets converged prior to November 2003, as seen earlier in Figure 4.2.

Starting in March 2004, the APOEs began building SSA-pure pallets for the highest-volume SSAs and consolidated other Army materiel on geographic region pallets. Once fully implemented in July, the RWT for shipments consolidated on APOE-built pallets again approached that of CCP shipments. Figure 4.7 reviews the types of pallets built by CCPs and APOEs over time.

The Benefits of SSA-Pure Multipacks and Pallets

There was a marked difference between RWTs and receipt rates for materiel shipped in SSA-pure multipacks and materiel shipped in mixed multipacks (of course, since RWT can only be measured for receipted items, it omits misshipments). Figure 4.8 provides a comparison. The column on the left has average RWT for materiel sent in TDC multipacks, with the receipt rate of just 63 percent on top of the column. The second column has shipments in 3rd Armored Cavalry Regiment (ACR) (ground SSA) multipacks for units in other divisions and the COSCOM. The third column, which has 3rd ACR materiel in 3rd ACR multipacks, contrasts sharply, with RWT close to two-thirds lower and a receipt rate of 94 percent. Two examples of SSA-pure

Figure 4.7
Configurations of Pallets by Consolidation Location

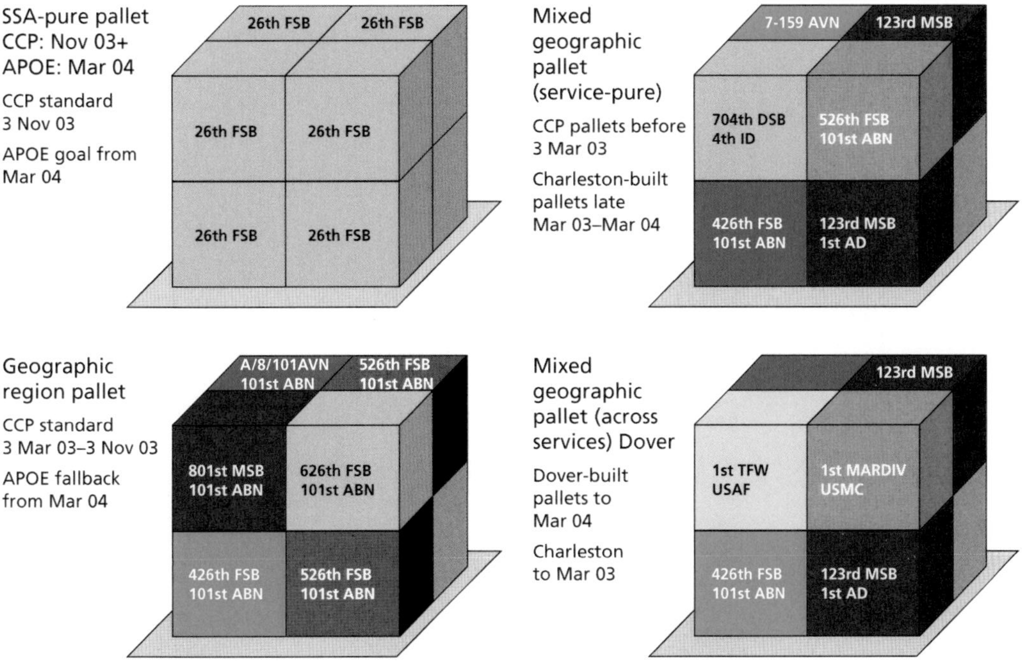

SSA-pure pallet
CCP: Nov 03+
APOE: Mar 04

CCP standard
3 Nov 03

APOE goal from
Mar 04

[Cube: 26th FSB, 26th FSB / 26th FSB, 26th FSB / 26th FSB, 26th FSB]

Mixed
geographic
pallet
(service-pure)

CCP pallets before
3 Mar 03

Charleston-built
pallets late
Mar 03–Mar 04

[Cube: 7-159 AVN, 123rd MSB / 704th DSB 4th ID, 526th FSB 101st ABN / 426th FSB 101st ABN, 123rd MSB 1st AD]

Geographic
region pallet

CCP standard
3 Mar 03–3 Nov 03

APOE fallback
from Mar 04

[Cube: A/8/101AVN 101st ABN, 526th FSB 101st ABN / 801st MSB 101st ABN, 626th FSB 101st ABN / 426th FSB 101st ABN, 526th FSB 101st ABN]

Mixed
geographic
pallet (across
services) Dover

Dover-built
pallets to
Mar 04

Charleston
to Mar 03

[Cube: 123rd MSB / 1st TFW USAF, 1st MARDIV USMC / 426th FSB 101st ABN, 123rd MSB 1st AD]

RAND *MG342-4.7*

multipacks are shown on the right: the 204th FSB in the 4th ID and the 584th Ordnance Company in the 3rd COSCOM.

Similarly, when pallets went from mixed to pure, the theater saw substantial improvement in theater distribution performance. Figure 4.9 compares the average theater distribution time for geographic region (but mixed across SSAs within the geographic region) pallets built by the CCP in October to the times for CCP SSA-pure pallets built in December. These are further divided into pallets shipped to Kuwait City International Airport (KCIA) and trucked into Iraq versus those flown directly into Balad northeast of Baghdad and where the corps distribution center (CDC) is located (the KCIA-bound pallets are first trucked to the CDC for inclusion in convoys to each SSA). The graphs show a savings of four to five days for the SSA-pure pallets. (While not shown here, a comparison of APOE-built pallets mixed across divisions and other geographic regions and SSA-pure pallets shows an even more dramatic difference, particularly as the mixed geographic region pallets have had low receipt rates comparable to the receipt rates for mixed SSA multipacks seen in Figure 4.8.)

Figure 4.8
Comparison of RWT and Receipt Rates Between Mixed and SSA-Pure Multipacks, Shipped and/or Closed by September

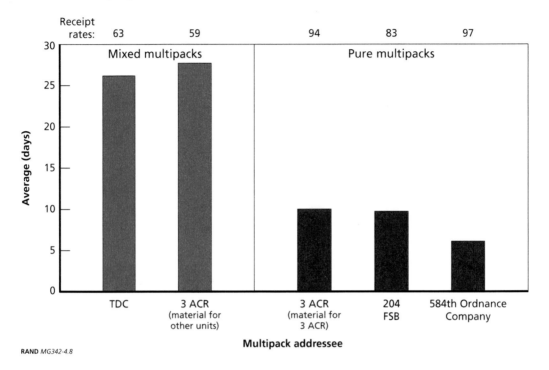

RAND *MG342-4.8*

Figure 4.9
RWT Comparison Between Mixed and SSA-Pure CCP Pallets, by APOD

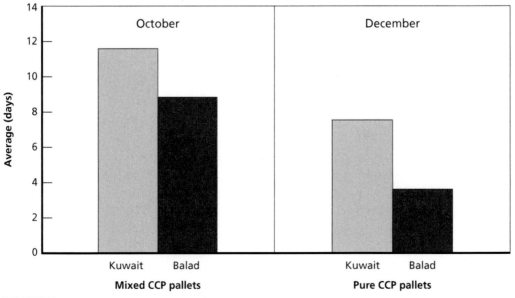

RAND *MG342-4.9*

Figure 4.10 reinforces the effect of pure pallets, but also illustrates that other factors have influenced theater distribution times. DLA implemented CCP-built SSA-pure pallets in November 2003, leading to an immediate improvement from October levels. Air Mobility Command began implementing a SSA-pure pallet strategy at Charleston AFB (for units in Iraq) and Dover AFB (for units in Kuwait) in March 2004. However, whereas DLA began virtually only SSA-pure pallets in a matter of days in November, implementation of a SSA-pure pallet policy at Air Mobility Command ports took longer, probably as the result of this being an entirely new APOE practice. SSA-pure pallets made up 60–80 percent of APOE-built pallets from March through June; only in July and afterwards did the success rate exceed 90 percent. One can see a dramatic divergence in theater times for shipments sent on CCP-built pallets as opposed to APOE-built pallets from November through February, some closing of the gap from March through June with the initial APOE implementation, and then an elimination of most of the gap in performance from July onward as the pallet-build practices became very similar.

Figure 4.10 also shows, though, that after March 2004, average theater distribution times, regardless of pallet-build source, turned higher, causing the overall upturn

Figure 4.10
Theater Distribution Time for Army Units in Iraq, by Month Departing CONUS, October 2003 to December 2004

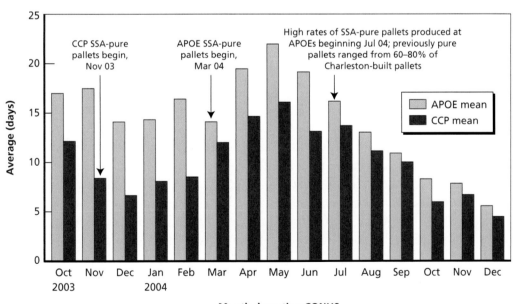

in RWT seen in the spring of 2004 in Figure 4.2. This degradation did not result from new problems in CONUS load consolidation. Rather, the growing intensity of the insurgency impeded theater distribution flows. Presumably, times would have been even higher if pallets and multipacks had still been mixed. There were also indications of some SSAs in OIF 2 after the major rotation of forces in early 2004 initially struggling in the effort to rapidly receipt their shipments. Over the course of several months, theater distribution operations were better tailored to the high threat environment and processes improved, resulting in theater times that continuously improved from June through December 2004, with particularly fast performance from October onward.

CONUS Distribution Center/CCP Capacity

Another serious problem hurting distribution performance was the inability of Defense Distribution Depot Susquehanna, PA (DDSP) to keep up with the unanticipated, sustained volume of demand flowing through the distribution center and the CCP. As the nation's SDP facing "east," it has been the primary distribution center and CCP for OIF, particularly for shipments to Army units. DDSP handled the volume during major combat operations fairly well through intensive surge operations. Demand stayed very high, though, through the summer and fall of 2003 and beyond as the size of the force grew and the operating pace remained fast, both beyond most expectations, to counter the growing Iraqi insurgency. With insufficient manpower to handle the incoming volume from May through August, times in the distribution center for issuing supplies, times at the CCP for receipting materiel coming into the CCP from outside of DDSP, and times in the CCP for building pallets all climbed greatly.

DLA took various steps to attack the problem of demand exceeding personnel capacity, including offloading some workload from DDSP. This was done in part by using two other distribution centers as CCPs for materiel being issued from them: the "west-facing" SDP at San Joaquin, California and the distribution center at Red River, Texas, which tends to store many of the heavy, bulky truck and tracked-vehicle parts such as tires and track shoes. Another means was to temporarily pass CCP-eligible cargo to APOEs, where it could be palletized by personnel there (but these were mixed pallets across divisions). The most critical step for working off the backlog that had accumulated at DDSP was to hire 400 "perm/term" employees to build up personnel capacity there. And, fortunately, demand did begin to fall by late 2003. In fact, by September 2003, it appears that DDSP had sufficient capacity to handle the incoming volume. The problem was that a substantial backlog had developed from May to August. To work off a backlog, though, an organization needs capacity that is greater than the demand level, which can be achieved by temporarily adding what is in actuality "excess" personnel capacity or waiting for demand to fall if that is a possibility. This "excess capacity" condition did not occur until the period from December to February 2004, which was when the backlog was worked off and performance returned to prewar levels. This shows how problematic it is to have a backlog develop in the midst of an operation, making it crucial to approve the requisite resources and rapidly adjust capacity, especially if demand will continue to be high for an extended period. This risk should be factored into the decision process for the approval of a request to implement a capacity expansion plan for contingencies. Of note, any shortfall in capacity, even a small one, can cause extended problems if the system never has a chance to "catch up." In this case, DDSP materiel release orders never exceeded capacity in any month by more than 8 percent.

Figure 4.11 shows the backlog development and recovery picture for the distribution center's operation at DDSP, what we earlier termed the warehouse operations segment of RWT. When the columns are positive, they show that materiel release orders (MROs) exceeded distribution center shipments for the month, indicative of a developing backlog. When the columns are negative, they show a backlog being worked off. The line/diamond series shows the average warehouse or pick/pack time by month of materiel release order.

Figure 4.11
DDSP Backlog Development and Warehouse Times

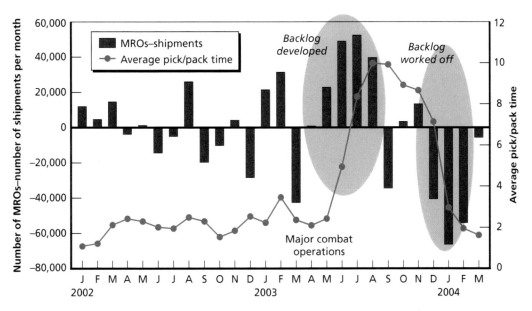

Recommendations

Within the realm of strategic distribution, the Army should work with its supply chain partners to shape the distribution system to ensure alignment with Army capabilities and requirements. While much of the distribution system is beyond formal Army control, the Army, as a major customer, should take an active role in the design of processes and organizations owned by non-Army organizations. The Army understands the needs and capabilities of its units in the field the best and so can bring unique expertise to the design of upstream capabilities. As the Army changes or develops unit capabilities and doctrine, it needs to ensure that this is done in concert with associated changes in the rest of the distribution system. To implement and maintain an integrated supply chain built around a common vision, there must be continual coordination and give-and-take that keeps organizational capabilities and processes aligned. Just as engineering product design organizations have found it inefficient and ineffective to throw their designs over the wall to manufacturing, turning instead to what is termed simultaneous engineering, so too the Army or its supply chain partners cannot throw their designs over the wall. Such practice extends development time and often results in less effective performance than employing simultaneous engineering from the start.

- The Army should work with USTRANSCOM as the distribution process owner (DPO) and DLA to ensure that single or SSA-pure multipacks and pallets are in joint policy. Formal agreements should be developed between the Army, USTRANSCOM, and DLA on how materiel should be configured for shipment. It is critical to ensure that peacetime practices and expectations are carried through to time of war for both integrated planning and effective execution, reflecting the maxim of "doing in peace what will be done in war."
- With DLA, the Army should work to develop mechanisms to ensure that DODAAC information and sortation logic remain up to date.
  - The Army and DLA should develop a standardized process for communicating DODAAC and support relationship changes and confirming the accuracy of associated changes in the DLA sortation logic.
  - DLA should improve its internal process for entering DODAAC and support relationship changes in DSS.
    - In the short term, SSA DODAAC changes should always be entered first, aided by the Army ensuring that it highlights SSA DODAAC changes for DLA.
    - In the long term, DLA should work toward automated entry into DSS of DODAAC and support relationship changes.
  - The Army should develop a standard deployment DODAAC policy with regard to whether home station DODAACs will be used upon deployment,

with changes of addresses, or whether the OIF (and Operation Enduring Freedom) practice of creating new deployment DODAACs will be the standard. Alternatively, the Army could choose to let the decision depend upon the conditions. Regardless, the policy chosen should be integrated into training and practiced when possible when units deploy from home station for training, to include combat training center deployments. This will exercise both unit processes for either changing addresses and DLA's systems for processing DODAAC and support relationship changes.

- As a customer, the Army should work with DLA to assess whether it has sufficiently rapid and adequate distribution center and CCP capacity expansion capabilities, and it should assist DLA in developing improved strategies for meeting contingency capacity requirements. The Army should work to provide DLA with accurate and detailed projected contingency demand requirements in terms of the overall level of demand, how fast the demands might increase, and how long they might continue. These requirements should then be compared to current DLA capabilities and contingency plans. Whether the "strict" two-SDP east/west strategy that was somewhat abandoned out of need in OIF should continue, whether the ad hoc use of multiple CCP operations for the support of one major contingency operation (as has been the case in OIF) should be formalized in contingency planning, or whether another strategy should be developed should be examined. A key question is whether or not both SDPs have to be capable of simultaneously supporting different major contingency operations.

With respect to the ramp-up of capacity within a distribution center, options should be explored. The first is how to expand the workforce more quickly. This could involve increased use of overtime, temporary transfers of personnel from other distribution centers, training process changes, changes in hiring practices, and labor contract changes. An alternative or complementary route would be the use of reserve component units trained for the mission. If pursued, this capability should be exercised, perhaps as part of annual training.

- The DPO, Air Mobility Command, and DLA, with the Army and the other services, should examine CCP bypass policy and coding: what role should aerial ports play? Analysis of shipments sent directly to APOEs to be put on pallets suggests that most such remaining shipments meet the CCP bypass criteria. Potential paths to improvement include upgrading APOE consolidation capabilities, increasing the capabilities and responsibilities of DLA so that DLA CCPs can build pallets for some of the materiel that bypasses the CCP (thus changing the bypass criteria and reducing or eliminating the need for APOE pallet building), or reviewing the bypass coding for accuracy to determine if some portion of the designated bypass items could be put on pallets by the CCP.

- Develop long-term aerial port pallet-build policies. The long-term policy development should be linked to the results of the bypass policy and coding analysis. Once the expected long-term APOE pallet-build volume is clear, a policy for future contingencies can be developed.

CHAPTER FIVE

National- and Theater-Level Inventory

In February 2003, a theater general support supply base, consisting of three central-ized theater SSAs holding common/ground spare parts, aviation spare parts, and Class II/IIIP/IV materiel, was set up in Kuwait. The intent was that when units needed materiel, the national supply system would first check this inventory before passing requests to be filled by sources outside of the theater.

Figure 5.1
Key National- and Theater-Level Inventory Characteristics in the Joint Supply Chain Vision (see pages 12–13)

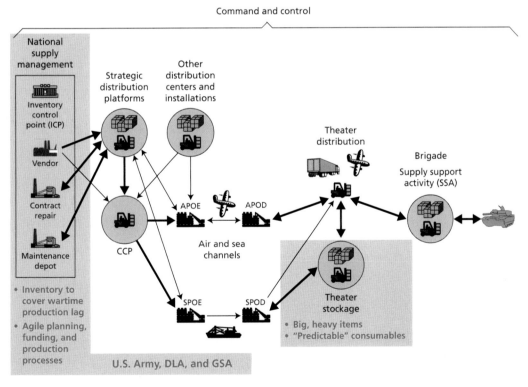

Ideally, theater stocks would hold most of the big, heavy items. But in OIF, forward positioned war reserves, held on land for conflict in Southwest Asia in Qatar and on board ships to "swing" to contingencies and used to initialize theater stocks for the two non-aviation GS SSAs (aviation spare parts are generally not in forward prepositioned stocks), were not effectively designed.[1] Nor was there a specific plan for the theater supply base to fulfill this purpose. Later, when it was desired to forward position these types of items to reduce airlift costs, it became difficult to do so, as national stocks had been depleted as a result of thin national war reserves combined with significant delays in the national production surge resulting from issues in the requirements determination and financial approval processes.

Backorder Rate for Army-Managed Items

Figure 5.2 shows the backorder rate for requisitions for Army-managed items (AMI) passed to the national supply system—that is, those that could not be filled by an ASL. In late 2003, the backorder rate skyrocketed, reaching 35 percent for the active Army in November as the Army ran low on a wide range of items.[2] The amount on the shelves when OIF started and any increase in procurements during that time was not enough.

Stepping through the backorder rate story from the beginning of 2002 through 2004 is instructive. Through the first half of 2002 the rate was steady at around 15 percent, the planned and budgeted rate. However, AMC began to approach the limits of its obligation authority (a financial management account that limits the total dollar value of orders AMC can place with external and internal suppliers—i.e., how much money it can commit) in the summer of 2002 and greatly slowed the placement of new orders. This slowdown in procurement appears to have led to the increased backorder rate late in the year. The lag effect reflects the fact that orders typically have a lead time of about three quarters of a year, with a range of a few months to two years. When replenishments are delayed due to a lack of funding, the backorders typically begin occurring a lead time beyond when the replenishment order should have been placed.

In October 2002, new fiscal year obligation authority (OA) became available, and AMC released to suppliers a large volume of "stacked" or deferred orders that

[1] The Army does not develop forward positioned war reserve requirements for aviation spare parts, but there were some aviation spare parts on hand in southwest Asia to support ongoing operations and training, which served as the initial basis for the aviation GS SSA.

[2] The backorder rate for DLA-managed spare parts ordered by Army units was about 8 percent early in 2002, rose to a peak of 13 percent in late 2003, and had recovered to 10 percent by mid-2004.

Figure 5.2
Backorder Rate for Army-Managed Spare Parts

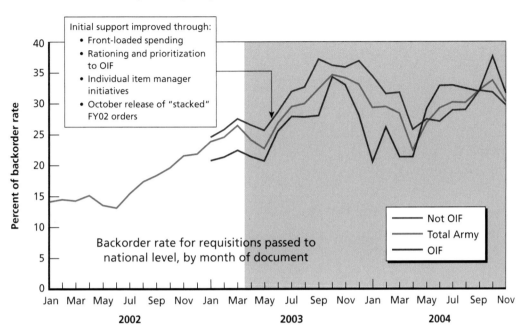

RAND *MG342-5.2*

had built up as the result of a financial shortfall in fiscal year 2002. Anticipating increased demand from the looming potential conflict, AMC used most of the full OA allotment for the total year in the first four months. Again, with the lead time, these orders started driving down the backorder rate in April and May 2003, just as major combat operations were ending and stability and support operations were beginning. Also during this period, the backorder rate for OIF units and non-OIF units diverged substantially as AMC item managers allocated items in short supply chiefly to OIF units.

However, the backorder rate started to rise in the summer of 2003 as demands began climbing due to the increasing scale and pace of stability operations. In the fall, they increased dramatically. Compounding the high demand was the fact that AMC greatly slowed the placing of orders from February through June, waiting for more OA. Not too surprisingly, several months down the road, when orders should have been coming in but were not because they could not be placed, the backorder rate rose sharply. Again, about six months or so after money started being committed to suppliers at a high rate in July and August of 2003, backorders began to come down somewhat but still remained relatively high, even ticking back up some. This pattern suggests that the forecasts that drove the funding increases provided in 2003 were insufficient to fully meet the high sustained demand.

Additionally, national war reserve inventory for spare parts was only designed to provide sustainment through the first 150 days of an operation. In OIF this five-month period passed before additional obligation authority to procure parts was released to meet the increased demands of the contingency, let alone before additional deliveries began coming in. Moreover, there were significant issues with the national war reserve sustainment stock requirements, and the requirements that were in place were poorly funded.

Beyond directly delaying the fulfillment of some maintenance requests, backorders also increase ASL replenishment times. Thus, they have become another factor hampering the recovery of ASL satisfaction and fill rates, which are critical for equipment readiness.

Air Shipping Costs

When national inventories become very low, parts must be saved for critical needs and it becomes impossible to fill the relatively slow, over-the-ocean surface pipeline. To ship materiel by surface requires sufficient inventory to fill the surface channel itself, which has ranged from 75 to 100 days to the theater supply base in Kuwait, while reserving some stock in the CONUS base to cover the possible need for emergency resupply by airlift. In OIF, therefore, most spare parts were provided by air, whether to directly satisfy maintenance requirements or to replenish inventory. These air shipments included big, heavy items that ideally would be sent by ship, e.g., tremendous amounts of track and tires. Airlift has also been used to ship relatively dense, high-demand items in other classes of supply that are generally more cost-effective to send by ship. The use of airlift proved necessary because national supplies were thin or the need was not identified soon enough. For example, in one short period in OIF, food had to be sent by air as national inventories became short, and food went directly from the production line to the field. Another example was the almost 200,000 cots for OIF 2 that were not requested early enough to send by ship.

The result has been over-reliance in OIF on airlift and much higher than desired air shipping costs. Figure 5.3 shows the monthly weight, shipping charges, and charges per pound for air shipments to Army forces in OIF. As demands to support stability operations increased, air shipping weight increased to about 25 million pounds per month from June through November 2003.

Moreover, the airlift charges rose even more than might have been expected because of an issue with how shipping charges are determined by Air Mobility Command. Through May, the standard APOD was KCIA and the rate to KCIA was based upon commercial benchmarks as a standard channel. However, in June, shipments started going to APODs in Iraq, and first Baghdad and then Balad became the

Figure 5.3
Monthly Air Shipping Weight, Charges, and Charges per Pound for Army Shipments

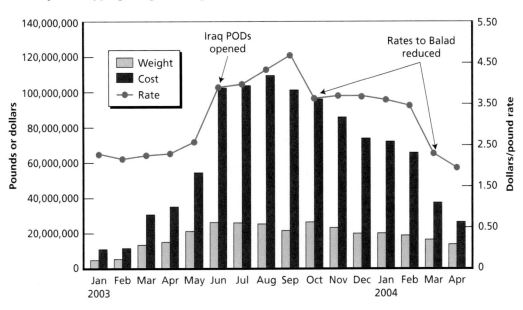

assigned APOD for units in Iraq. The routes to these APODs were so-called contingency routes with charges set by a different method. The result was a price per pound that doubled as the mix of unit locations changed from April to September, and of course, along with this, the total charges doubled from what might have been expected solely from the change in weight. When DoD financial managers realized that AMC was bringing too much money into the Transportation Working Capital Fund through what had become its highest-volume sustainment air channel, rates were reduced to "commercial equivalents" in March 2004. The combined result of the swings in weight and shipping rates was an increase in monthly charges from $30 million in March to a peak of $110 million in August and back down to less than $30 million in April 2004. Issues with how shipping rates are calculated have been recognized by Air Mobility Command and USTRANSCOM, and a new system is being established that will prevent such wild swings in the future.

The very high charges for airlift to Iraq did draw significant attention at the top levels of the Army, putting tremendous pressure on the Army's logisticians to find ways to reduce air shipping costs. This pressure produced many ideas, some of which might have significantly hampered support, such as shipping all replenishments to ASLs via ocean shipments, which would have meant at least a tripling of replenishment times. In the end, though, it provided impetus to take the action of revising the breadth and depth of GS theater inventory requirements to place the appropriate amount of big, heavy items there in accordance with the joint supply chain vision described in Chapter One. Some items will have to wait for sufficient national stocks to have sufficient inventory in Kuwait to enable utilization of the long ocean pipeline, but changes are headed in the right direction. DLA also established a forward distribution center in Kuwait in late 2004, called a theater distribution platform, focused on airlift reduction, with stockage focused on the highest-volume DLA-managed items in terms of weight and cube.

Army Prepositioned Sustainment Stocks

Army Prepositioned Stock (APS) war reserve sustainment stocks (AWRS stocks) consist of major end items to replace combat losses and war reserve secondary items (WRSI), which consist of spare parts, other expendable materiel (e.g., clothing), and subsistence items, stored for use in regional contingencies. Sustainment stocks positioned in CONUS (referred to as APS-1) are intended to cover contingency demand rates above the level that can be supported from "peacetime"-based inventory levels until the production base can surge. Forward positioned sustainment stocks are intended to provide sufficient stocks in the area of operations to cover demand until the sea lines of communication are opened and resupply can be established. These are land-based in critical regions and afloat to provide flexibility. For OIF, theater sustainment stocks of spare parts positioned in Qatar (APS-5) and aboard two container ships (APS-3) were made available to support operations. One of the two ships had been designated to support contingencies in Southwest Asia and one had been designated for Northeast Asia, but they had very similar inventory configurations and are considered "swing" stocks.

Forward Positioned WRSI

The concept used to produce the guidance given for the computation of forward positioned WRSI in APS-3 and APS-5 was to have enough inventory to cover theater demands for the first 60 days, conceived of as the expected time needed to open the sea LOC, and implying that the first ocean shipments should be expected to arrive on day 61 of operations. They were not clearly designed as the basis of GS theater inventory that would be replenished as it is consumed—or what we might term "starter" stocks. Nor does it appear that their design was integrated with theater replenishment plans.

The concept had several flaws. The first is that the concept assumes that almost every "mission-essential" item, as identified by essentiality codes, that could *potentially* be demanded should be forward positioned. The second is an implicit assumption that airlift will not be available to provide any of these items during the initial 60 days of operations. The third is an implied lack of integration with resupply plans from the way in which the inventory levels were set and defined.

There were also several problems with how this flawed concept was implemented. The first has to do with flaws in the computations that determined the requirements for spare parts in a contingency. Second, inventory was not configured on land or on ships in a way that would make it easy to manage and issue the spare parts in the first portion of an operation if there were real delay in providing supplies by air or sea. Third, appropriate inventory management parameters were not computed and stored for data transfer to a theater SSA.

By failing to sharply focus on parts that drive equipment readiness and by disregarding the potential contribution of airlift, the requirements computations created excessive requirements for forward positioning, with requirements generated for a tremendous number of items. With respect to spare parts, the theater land stocks had requirements for over 50,000 different parts, and the afloat inventory had requirements for over 20,000.[3] Almost half of the parts with forward positioned requirements were not demanded in calendar year 2003 by units involved in OIF, to include preparation for operations. Over two-thirds of the items without demands were "insurance items" that do not have enough worldwide demands across the services in normal operations to qualify for *national* inventory based upon standard demand criteria. However, national inventory does include many of these relatively slow-moving or inactive parts, especially those with long procurement lead times, as "just in case" insurance items, and the quantity held in national inventory in CONUS for many of them is greater than the WRSI requirement. Since CONUS baseline stocks can offset CONUS war reserve requirements, if these insurance items did not have a forward positioned requirement, they would not have a WRSI requirement at all. They would simply be covered by standard stocks. Then in the rare instances when they are demanded, most could easily be flown, with almost no effect on airlift consumption, because most of these items are very small. For example, the total forward positioned requirement computed for 40,000 of the APS-5 items had an extended cube or space requirement less than that of a single shipping container.

The true cost of having forward positioned requirements for a large number of small items was in the workload associated with setting up and operating a warehouse with such a large number of locations. A warehouse with 50,000 storage locations is difficult to manage and requires a fairly large operation in terms of facilities and personnel. Such a warehouse would not be conducive to effective operations with a small "footprint" in the beginning stages of a contingency.

Despite their tremendous number, the items in the APS forward positioned requirements, if resourced, would have done a relatively poor job of accommodating

---

[3] The land portion of the requirement was intended to cover the first 45 days with the ships covering an additional 15 days to get to 60 days. If the quantity required during the first 45 days was also enough to cover the full 60 days, then afloat stocks would not have a requirement for an item. This will usually happen with very-low-demand items for which the quantity of inventory for a specific part required to achieve readiness goals does not change between 45 and 60 days.

OIF demands for spare parts as well as for packaged POL products, engineer materiel, and items in other classes of supply deemed critical. For spares, this holds
whether one looks at just readiness drivers, the total population of parts that are
coded as mission essential (the basis for the requirements), or all spare parts.

Figure 5.4 shows the proportion of parts with forward positioned requirements
that were actually demanded in 2003 by Army units in OIF. Most of the parts are
small and inexpensive, and the majority of them have not been seen to deadline a
piece of Army equipment in the last three years. With 50,000 parts, the vast majority
of spare part demands in OIF should have been covered by the requirements if the
parts had been chosen reasonably well. As the population is thinned first to mission-
essential items and then to the relatively small population of readiness drivers, these
should have been almost completely covered. Instead the requirements for APS-3 and
APS-5 covered just over 30 percent and 55–60 percent of demands for readiness
drivers, respectively. Figure 5.5 compares the accommodation rate for the forward
positioned requirements in terms of all spare parts and readiness drivers to the proportion of demands in OIF stemming from increasing numbers of parts, starting
with the highest-demand part and adding parts in order of their contribution to the
percentage of demands. In effect, the lines in Figure 5.5 represent what might be
called an "efficient frontier" or the set of points representing the best achievable accommodation rates as the number of parts is increased. The reasons for the disparity

Figure 5.4
Spare Parts Requirements for Forward Positioned War Reserve

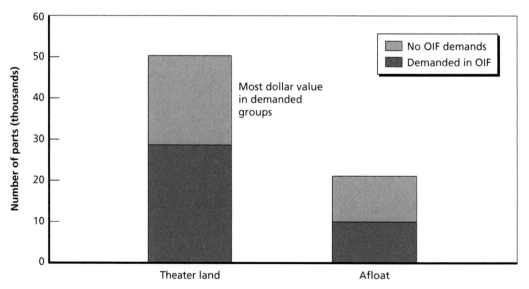

Figure 5.5
Accommodation Rate of Forward Positioned AWRS Versus OIF Demands in All of 2003
Compared to the "Efficient Frontier"

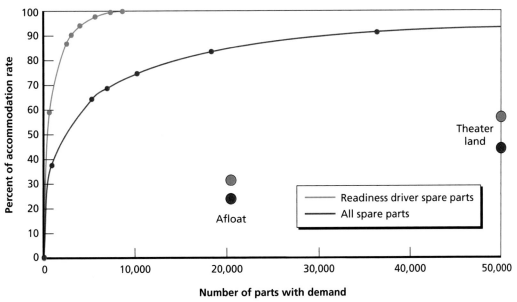

RAND *MG342-5.5*

between the "efficient frontier" and the OIF accommodation rate for the requirements appear to arise primarily from data filtering and input problems. In particular, the data used to make the requirements computations excluded consideration of many parts that have been shown to deadline end items.

Nor did the forward positioned WRSI requirements do a good job of including parts that would be inordinately expensive to ship by air, thus serving as "starter" general support theater stocks for such items. Figure 5.6 shows that of the 1,325 items that contributed the most to air shipping costs in OIF, 88 percent had either no forward positioned requirement or an insufficient required quantity to cover replenishment by ship, based upon a 60-day replenishment time (which is faster than has been achieved to date in OIF for ocean shipments).[4]

Only about 6 percent of the requirements in APS-5 and APS-1 for spare parts were resourced. Of that, almost 90 percent of the dollar value of APS-5 spare parts was positioned in CONUS versus forward in theater. The level of resourcing for the other classes of supply was similar, and the malpositioning was worse. APS-3 was suf-

---

[4] $50,000 in air shipment charges was used as a cutoff. This was based upon actual charges prior to the Air Mobility Command price reduction in March 2004.

Figure 5.6
Comparison of APS Forward Positioned Required Quantities to the 60-Day Quantities of the Top 1,325 Airlift Drivers in OIF

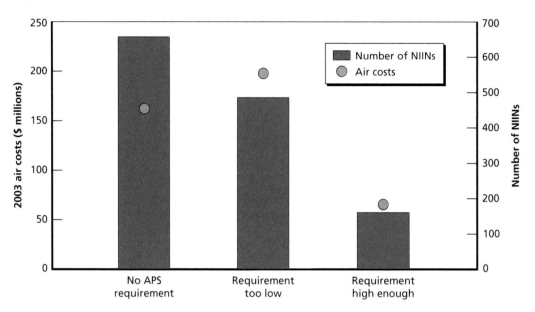

ficiently funded to fill the two container ships, though, and the assets were appropriately positioned on the ships. However, the on-hand spare part assets in APS-3 represented only 20 to 25 percent of the requirement.[5]

Since forward positioned war reserve is intended to cover the first 60 days of operations, it should be easy for a unit to deploy, fall in on the "warehouse," and begin to provide supplies to units in the theater. However, the materiel on the APS sustainment ships was not configured in storage to support a "turnkey" startup. Rather, many different items were often stored in one container, with an entire container having what is known as just one storage location. Inside the containers there were generally not separate shelves, bins, or other means for establishing separate physical locations either. For warehouse personnel to be able to find an item when it is ordered, each item must have its own location. So if the Army would want to use the forward positioned WRSI stock containers as an expeditionary warehouse, instead of having to take the time to unload them and set up a new warehouse, the storage locations inside the containers would have be configured to enable easy access to each different item stored therein. Additionally, the information system that had been used to account for the inventory in storage was not the same as and was not fully compatible with the information system operated by the field Army and used by the

---

[5] However, the full APS-3 requirement would not have fit on the ships.

units that ran the general support SSAs in Kuwait. These factors combined with theater startup problems to delay the initiation of effective GS supply support.

Finally, to be effective, forward inventory quantities and management must be tightly tied to national inventory and strategic distribution planning. This is the case for both tactical ASLs and theater stockage. The way the Army inventory system is designed, depending upon a host of factors such as the cost of an item and how long it takes to send a replenishment shipment, two parameters must be determined. The first is the point at which a replenishment shipment should be sent. This is called the ROP. For the theater stockage, one can generally think of this level of inventory as the amount that is expected to be consumed over the time it takes for a replenishment shipment to arrive plus some margin of safety stock to account for variability. The other parameter is how much to order for each replenishment. In the Army system, this results in a RO. When inventory falls below the ROP, the system submits an order equivalent to the RO less the current inventory position.

Thus, if the forward positioned stocks are to serve as a "starter" for a general support theater supply base meant to continue operations beyond the first 60 days, the RO and ROP are needed for every item. However, no such parameters were associated with forward positioned WRSI. In effect, though, the required quantities represent a ROP, as they reflect expected consumption until the sea LOCs are opened, which can be interpreted as when the first replenishment arrives. If this is the case and the Army wants the theater supply to continue to provide these items after the first 60 days, then when the items are brought into theater inventory, they would be initially at the ROP, signaling the need for an immediate replenishment. That is, a replenishment should be sent by ship on the day that the theater supply initiates operations, and it should arrive within 60 days. If the desire were to enable a delay in when the first replenishment departed, for example to devote early shipping to unit deployments, the inventory requirement for forward positioned stock would have to be above the level needed in the first 60 days (assuming that remains as the expected surface replenishment time) or greater than the ROP. It should be noted that the surface replenishment time to the GS theater base in OIF has been greater than 60 days throughout OIF.

Either way, the general support supply units need to know the ROs and ROPs in order to know when to order replenishments and how much to order. In OIF, lacking this information, when supply personnel incorporated the sustainment stocks into the theater stocks, they set the ROs to the on-hand levels in forward positioned war reserve, with the ROPs set arbitrarily to 70 percent of these levels. These two parameters had to be established and entered in the Standard Army Retail Supply System (SARSS) in order to operate the GS SSAs. As per the previous discussion, given the way the forward positioned levels were computed, it would have been more appropriate to set the ROPs at the on-hand levels (or higher if the on-hand levels were less than the requirements). Ideally, the war reserve information system should have a

RO and ROP for each item that can be transferred to the information system used by the GS supply unit.

When all of these factors are combined, the result is relatively little value produced by theater stockage with respect to expectations or its potential. For example, about 16,000 different spare parts (different stock numbers) were actually positioned forward, primarily on the ships. These parts were removed from the containers and set up in individual storage locations in a fixed warehouse facility in Kuwait, a time-consuming process. This inventory did little to reduce the consumption of airlift to satisfy sustainment needs, and most of the original 16,000 lines were later removed from the GS base ASL due to either no demands, low demands, or lack of criticality to the theater. As indicated above, the majority of readiness and airlift drivers were not forward positioned. Figure 5.7 repeats the accommodation rate versus efficient frontier curves shown earlier, but now with respect to the items that had on-hand levels of spare parts on the sustainment ships and that were brought into theater inventory. The land-based forward positioned sustainment stock was virtually nonexistent, because the requirements were not resourced.

Adjustments were made to improve upon the initial theater inventory by various personnel during OIF, but this was done without clear guidance on what the role

Figure 5.7
Accommodation Rate of Items Actually On Hand in Forward Positioned War Reserve Versus the Efficient Frontiers

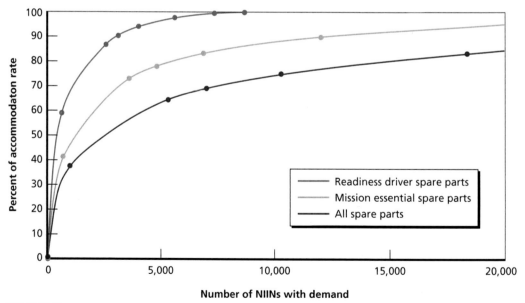

RAND *MG342-5.7*

of the theater inventory should be. Doctrine does not provide a guide, and there were different conceptions of its role and how inventory items and quantities should be selected. Consequently, many of the same big, heavy items consistently contributed to heavy sustainment airlift requirements from early in OIF through the summer of 2004. In June 2004, the Army Materiel Command and CFLCC directed changes to the inventory composition of the GS SSAs intended to reduce airlift consumption and cost. This consisted of adding "missing" airlift drivers and increasing the quantities of those that were already stocked. Then in the fall of 2004, DLA opened a forward distribution center in Kuwait to stock DLA-managed airlift drivers. The AMC and CFLCC plan is to draw down the inventory in the GS SSA and establish inventory of AMC-managed big, heavy items in the DLA distribution center.

CONUS-Based War Reserve Sustainment Stocks

Conceptually, CONUS-based WRSI in APS-1 was much better aligned with an appropriate role for contingency operations such as OIF. The role of APS-1 is to ensure that contingency demand rates can be met until production and inventory can be increased sufficiently to meet wartime demands. As opposed to forward positioned stocks, it should include insurance items that units should not have to wait months or even more than a year to receive. Rather, if a small number are held in CONUS, they can be provided rapidly by strategic air. Again, many such items are offset by peacetime stock levels.

APS-1 did have two sets of problems in common with forward positioned war reserve: requirements determination execution problems and a very low level of funding. Primarily due to data issues, the items with APS-1 requirements had a relatively low accommodation rate against total theater demands for Army units in OIF, only accommodating a little over half of the requests for spare parts that appear on Army deadline reports. This means that many readiness drivers in OIF had no CONUS-based war reserve requirement.

For OIF, required quantities were also insufficient in many cases. The first factor is again an issue with data—specifically, failure-rate data. The second factor is that Department of the Army guidance called for computing requirements for war reserves out to 150 days. It is not clear whether this guidance assumed that an operation would be over by that point or at least that demands would be relatively low after 150 days, or if it was believed that the industrial base could fully respond by that time. In OIF, this period of 150 days extended through May 2003, as it is not based upon the start of combat operations but the start of operations. Demands were just gaining steam at that point in OIF, and additional obligation authority for suppliers to increase production and deliveries had not even been provided to AMC at that point. Add the average lead time for spare parts of nine to ten months, and one can see the extent of the disconnects between war reserve concepts, Army guidance on war reserve requirements determination, war reserve funding, and delayed approval and funding for AMC to increase supplies.

Determining and Resourcing National-Level Requirements for Spare Parts

Before AMC can increase production and national inventory to support a contingency operation, two connected processes have to be completed. The first is determining the spare parts requirements for the contingency, and the second is the approval and release of additional Army Working Capital Fund (AWCF) Supply Management Army (SMA) obligation authority (OA). The OA is needed to permit Army Materiel Command item managers to let contracts and place depot repair orders or, in other words, to commit money to suppliers in order to procure and repair spare parts. The use of OA is a promise by AMC to pay its suppliers cash upon delivery, cash that AMC generates by selling parts to Army units and other AWCF customers. Army units pay AMC for the items through appropriated operations and maintenance dollars.

With the war reserve shortfalls created by the problems with APS WRSI requirements and resourcing, the ability to rapidly assess and resource OIF spare parts requirements was critical. In the case of OIF, given the limited on-hand WRSI stocks, these activities should have been completed by the fall of 2002 to offset the procurement lead times for most parts. In fact, this was when AMC developed the initial estimates of how increased demand rates would affect AMC requirements and the associated need for increased OA. Even without problems with WRSI requirements determination and funding, this would have been the appropriate time for increasing OA, as WRSI guidance was to cover only the first 150 days of operations.[6] However, it took until June 2003 for the first installment of increased OA associated with OIF requirements to be released to AMC,[7] with the total estimated required increase not provided until September 2003.[8] This meant that most contingency-based orders began to arrive anywhere from nine months to more than two years after the start of operations, with a year plus typical.

Financial processes must be highly proactive to support a contingency effectively; this means that they should be able to accommodate some of the financial risk associated with beginning to support a contingency that is still in the planning

---

[6] Jeff Landis, U.S. Army Materiel Systems Analysis Activity, "War Reserve and Iraqi Freedom Demands," briefing, 5 November 2003.

[7] As described later, large OA increases earlier in the year were associated with a shortfall in the "baseline" or peacetime budget.

[8] Office of the Deputy Chief of Staff, G-3, AMC, "FY03 AMC AWCF Releases Close-v3.0," spreadsheet.

phases. While demands associated with OIF peaked in the summer of 2003, about the time of the initial increase in OA, there is a delay associated with administrative and production or repair lead times before the availability of stocks will increase. These administrative and production lead times have averaged about 10 months in the OIF time frame.[9] So only if the Army and DoD had a very rapid process for requirements determination and financial approval would it have been possible to have at least some parts coming in from suppliers at higher levels by the time supplies had started to run thin.

The first cause of the late OA was delayed validation of the requirement by Headquarters, Department of the Army (HQDA), which can be attributed to process problems in both requirements determination and financial approval. Analysis of these processes suggests several underlying issues. No formal contingency planning guidance was given to AMC. While AMC had information about the potential OIF contingency, neither CENTCOM nor HQDA, which approves and releases OA to AMC after getting approval from the Office of the Secretary of Defense (OSD), provided AMC with official planning guidance regarding force size, composition, and operating tempo.[10] As a result, the Office of the Deputy Chief of Staff, G-3, AMC came up with the planning assumptions required to develop spare parts requirements for OIF, first in November 2002 and then in March 2003.[11] While the assumptions turned out to be relatively accurate and reflective of the war plan, it is not clear that the assumptions had the buy-in of HQDA. Also, both HQDA and OSD seem to have initially discounted one or more assumptions about the scale, length, and operating tempo of the operation, seemingly below that of even the operational plan developed by CENTCOM.[12]

From these assumptions, AMC developed aggregate estimates for funding increases, which were presented to HQDA.[13] However, detailed requirements for specific parts were developed through a separate bottom-up, decentralized process executed without systematic application of contingency planning factors derived from the assumptions used to develop the aggregate estimate. In other words, different AMC subordinate commands and even business units and item managers, within commands, used different planning factors, and even forecasting methodologies, to determine OIF requirements.[14] When AMC initially brought the aggregate budget

---

[9] Office of the Deputy Chief of Staff, G-3, AMC, "030603 inventory update v3," briefing.

[10] Interview with Mr. William Mullen, Office of the DCS, G-3, AMC by Eric Peltz.

[11] Interview with Mr. William Mullen, Office of the DCS, G-3, AMC, "030611 budget audit trail v4," spreadsheet.

[12] Based upon discussions with personnel in the Army Budget Office and Office of the Deputy Chief of Staff, G-8, HQDA and review of the CENTOM operational plan.

[13] Office of the DCS, G-3, AMC, "030611 budget audit trail v4," spreadsheet.

[14] Interviews with AMC item managers and system analysts.

estimate to HQDA, it was rejected for insufficient justification, initiating an iterative loop of questioning and justification that was largely unavoidable given the disconnect between the bottom-up and aggregate budget level estimates produced by AMC.[15] A clean audit trail from requirements to war plans did not exist, so the discussion revolved more around how the requirements were computed than on the assumptions about the potential upcoming contingency and what level of operations should be planned for. Additionally, changes in the budget estimate were made as assumptions were adjusted based upon new information and changes in contingency expectations, again without formal guidance from outside of AMC.

Adding to the iterative nature of the process was an apparent overemphasis on reducing financial risk (will the Army buy too much, as might happen if the operation is completed more quickly and easily than expected?) and an underemphasis on reducing the operational risk, which is not formally quantified, associated with the parts not being available to maintain the deployed equipment. Additionally, it does not appear that knowledge about shortfalls in APS WRSI, which was to cover the increased demands until production and repair could ramp up, entered into the validation process.

From AMC's first estimate of the contingency requirement for spare parts in November 2002, it took until March 2003, when operations commenced, for the Office of the Deputy Chief of Staff, G-3, AMC to "validate" the requirements submitted by each of its subordinate commands as one consolidated OA requirement. March also marks the first recognition of a need for increased obligation authority at HQDA. In April, AMC validated another large requirements increase, with additional increases coming in July through September 2003. "Validated" is in quotation marks because there is not an official validation of requirements change outside of the formal planning, programming, budgeting, and execution (PPBE) process that sets long-term and annual budgets. Approval and release of the OA to AMC lagged another three months beyond the March and April requirements validations to June and July respectively, with a third major OA increase in August 2003, reflecting time lags in the financial approval and OA release process.[16]

When an increase in demand is modest and demand returns to normal quickly, a failure to promptly increase OA can be offset by prioritizing which units get parts and accelerating the commitment of existing OA to speed up deliveries of parts. Part shortfalls would then affect units involved in post-conflict reset and training. In fact, the success of such tactics in the past may have contributed to the delays in recognizing the increased requirements, and AMC used both of these tactics to mitigate the effects of the delayed release of OA. Initially, through prioritization, backorder

---

[15] Interview with Mr. Gary Motsek, Deputy to the DCS, G-3, AMC by Eric Peltz and LTC Jeff Angers.

[16] Office of the Deputy Chief of Staff, G-3, AMC, "FY03 AMC AWCF Releases Close-v3.0," spreadsheet.

Collate Color Text Section

Collate Color Text Section

the amount of orders released to internal and external suppliers. The monthly commitments are relatively in line with what one might expect in advance of a large contingency from October to January, but then they slow dramatically through June or July as AMC had approached its OA limits. AMC was reluctant to fully exhaust its OA before it was certain that OA would be increased later in the year, wanting instead to save and prioritize commitments for future high-priority needs.

Financial risk to the AWCF stems from the possibility of committing money to suppliers and then not having sufficient cash on hand to pay the suppliers when the items are delivered and payment is due. Thus, this produces the reluctance to provide more OA to AMC when the timing and scale of a contingency's demands are uncertain. There is a way around this risk: giving cash infusions to AMC up front to buy more parts protects against the possibility of insolvency. This, though, requires the use of appropriated funds in advance of the contingency. This tactic was implemented to a limited degree for OIF, but not until the summer of 2003, with dollars earmarked for specific items. Alternatively, the risk can be taken recognizing that potential insolvency may require a cash infusion later, depending on the contingency's demands and how much OA is increased and committed against up front.

Recommendations

- Develop doctrine and associated policy for theater stockage that limit inventory requirements for forward positioned items to those items that drive readiness or consume substantial airlift and that are cost-effective to stock forward at surface replenishment depth (i.e., high ratio of shipping cost to purchase cost).
  - Integrate with APS forward positioned WRSI policy and requirements determination.
  - Limit APS insurance items to CONUS-based war reserves.
  - Generally set inventory levels to support surface replenishment.
    - Reduce surface replenishment times.
  - Consider including small or expensive readiness drivers in forward stockage with the depth requirement based upon air replenishment in those cases in which theater lateral time is substantially faster than strategic distribution. It should be noted, though, that this will often not be the case. For instance, in OIF, lateral distribution has generally not offered an advantage over strategic distribution.[20] Another reason to consider including such items in forward stockage would be to protect against strategic distribution disruptions.

---

[20] In OIF, however, units sometimes go to the warehouse themselves to pick up an item from the GS theater stockage, which can produce a time advantage.

- Improve the APS requirements determination methodology.[21]
  - Improve the use of empirical data for determining equipment failure rates and identifying the parts that drive equipment readiness. Too many readiness and airlift drivers are being excluded.
  - Incorporate cost and storage constraints into requirements computations to produce automated prioritization.
  - Compute ROs and ROPs for forward positioned requirements.
- Improve the storage of forward positioned WRSI to support a smoother transition to war. Make the APS WRSI into turnkey GS SSAs to reduce early workload in theater and to better support expeditionary operations.
  - Ensure that the information system for inventory accounting is fully compatible with the field system, to include the ability to transfer ROs, ROPs, and inventory position information.
  - Store each item in a separate location in containers, which should be configured for use as an operational warehouse.
- Develop a standard, accurate, and fast process for changing requirements and allocating obligation authority for national inventory increases and a production surge, as needed, to support contingencies as they are planned and subsequently evolve.
  - The regional combatant command should provide scenario planning guidance to HQDA.
  - HQDA should provide AMC with official guidance on assumptions for the development of contingency demand forecasts for use in determining inventory and production requirements.
  - AMC G-3 should direct its subordinate commands to employ specified logistics planning factors based upon the HQDA scenario planning guidance in their inventory models. Longer term, the planning factors might be centrally input.
  - An aggregate forecast of need then should be developed from a bottom-up rollup.
  - A process should be in place to execute steps 1 through 4 rapidly.
  - Apply risk management techniques for contingency budget approval.
    - High-payoff, low-financial-risk buys: these are readiness items with relatively high demand and low variability. Even if consumption is delayed,

---

[21] The methodology for WRSI is similar to that for computing APS ASL requirements, and many of the same recommendations apply.

they will generally be used. The future value of the inventory for these items tends to be relatively high.

- ♦ Critical, long-lead items: not ordering these items early can lead to significant operational risk.

- ♦ Multi-scenario consideration: the combatant command and HQDA scenario input and planning guidance should cover a range of possibilities rather than forcing the process to work from single-point estimates. Then the decision process should focus on the likelihood of the various scenarios and the operational risk associated with not protecting against each. For each scenario, the parts in the high-payoff, low-financial-risk and critical, long-lead categories and their requirements should be separately identified.

- ♦ The decision process should then change from "yes or no?" to "how much?" based upon judgments of allowable levels of financial and operational risk. Decisionmakers would be presented with a range of options, with rough probabilities and risk assessments provided for each.

- – Review the requirements review, financial approval, and obligation authority release processes to identify opportunities for improving process speed, leveraging the risk management approach and requirements determination process improvements stemming from the recommendations described above.

- Conduct AMC and HQDA exercises to produce and review contingency requirements and to execute the financial approval process.

- Continue and accelerate efforts to reduce administrative, production, and repair lead times in order to reduce AMC's replenishment lead times. The more these times can be reduced, the smaller the tradeoffs that must be made between operational and financial risk. The risks are reduced and the tradeoffs are both simpler and less critical; mistakes can be corrected. Decisions to commit money to suppliers for increased production can be made closer to the start of a contingency.

rates for Army-managed items for units not deployed in OIF were substantially higher than for units in OIF, as seen in Figure 5.2. Also, AMC leadership assumed that the OIF spare parts requirements would be validated and funded, and they obligated OA intended for the entire fiscal year to procurement and repair at a very high rate from October 2002 through January 2003, perhaps close to the rate really needed to support operations. However, as delays in approval of increased OA stretched out into the next calendar year, monetary commitments to suppliers were limited from February through June 2003. Once these commitments approached the approved limit on OA, AMC held back some procurement orders in anticipation of more critical ones later in the year that could not have been executed if OA were not increased. For example, a very critical part might be projected to hit its reorder point in another month or two. In this case, orders for some less critical parts would be held. Decreased obligation execution combined with the procurement and repair lead-time lag effect contributed to a continually increasing backorder rate from June through November, with improving but still high backorder rates through April 2004.[17] However, at that point, the backorder rate began climbing again until October. Analysis of AMC inventory requirements over time and supply performance suggests that the forecasts made in 2003 for the requirements increases were insufficient. Thus, even the seemingly large OA increases in 2003 were not enough to build inventory to the level needed to support the continuing high-intensity counterinsurgency operation in conjunction with home station reset and training demands.

Figure 5.8 provides the numbers behind much of this account. The shaded steps show the various levels of approved spare parts (hardware) requirements for the 2003 fiscal year. The year actually started at a budgeted level of just under $3 billion, which presented the first problem—in effect, the Army began in a financial hole (similarly, recall the limited resourcing of the WRSI requirements).[18] Due to increasing demands at the national level over the previous several years and a lengthy PPBE process that results in budgets based upon data that are one to three years old

---

[17] A FY02 OA shortfall led to similar procurement and repair stops late in the fiscal year. These led to increasing backorder rates a lead-time away from November 2002 to March 2003. For undetermined reasons, baseline demands had increased steadily from 1999 to 2002. This dynamic demand pattern is not well accommodated by the PPBE process, as the budget is typically based upon two-year-old data and change is difficult. Thus, 2002's budget, based upon demands through September 2000, was low. The peacetime budget for 2003 was similarly low. It was adjusted upward in December. This December 2003 change introduced confusion into the process, as it was assumed by some to have been for OIF. Instead it was primarily to accommodate a low FY03 peacetime forecast. However, it also probably included some changes by individual item managers to account for CONOPS. The confusion resulted from an inability to fully separate these through a systematic planning process and audit trail.

[18] The Army also began the year with a procurement and repair backlog, as orders were delayed in late fiscal year 2002 when AMC ran out of OA, and thus a looming supply availability hole that showed up in the increasing backorder rate early in fiscal year 2003 before OIF began.

Figure 5.8
OIF AMC Spare Parts Requirements, Funding, and OA Execution

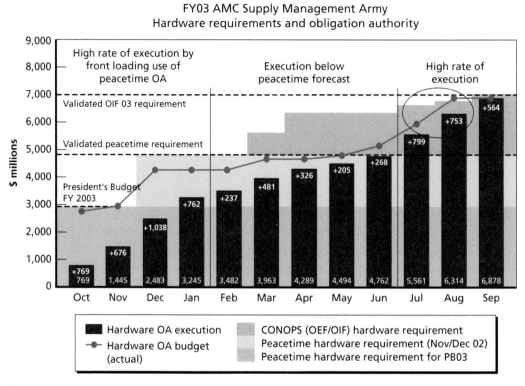

and potentially older by the start of the year of execution, in this dynamic situation the budget and the requirement were significantly misaligned. AMC worked with HQDA to revise the baseline requirements and OA, which were both increased by close to $2 billion. In retrospect, it is apparent that some personnel involved in the approval process associated this increase with OIF requirements, which most likely impeded approvals for further increases when the OIF requests came in, which first occurred at about the same time as the baseline or "peacetime" increase.[19] In actuality, this increase can be justified through a backward-looking view. The two other major steps in requirements increases are in March and April, when combat operations began. Ideally these steps would have occurred earlier. The line series marked by diamonds reflects the approved OA limit for the year by month, with major increases in December for the baseline adjustment and then June through August for OIF. The columns portray the amount of OA execution by month by AMC. This is

---

[19] Interviews with personnel in the Office of the Deputy Chief of Staff, G-8, Department of the Army and the Army Budget Office.

CHAPTER SIX

Command and Control

Good logistics situational awareness promises to aid decisionmaking by logistics system customers and help logistics system managers quickly detect and correct problems. Conversely, a lack of good situational awareness and effective process monitoring and control systems led to the delays in resolving many of the OIF sustainment problems discussed in Chapters Two through Five. Additionally, limited situational awareness affected risk assessments by commanders and their staffs in the decisionmaking process during combat operations. While they do not appear to have altered operational decisions in OIF, the deficiencies could potentially be important in future contingencies. Additionally, a lack of detailed logistics situational awareness by end consumers in the supply chain makes it difficult for them to assess their ordering (and reordering) requirements, which will tend to cause them to order and "hoard" additional materiel.

Limited Situational Awareness During Combat Operations

The U.S. Army and the Department of Defense at large came into OIF in the midst of an evolution toward better situational awareness tools and the fielding of systems to provide in-transit visibility (ITV) of supplies to enhance this situational awareness. Different portions of the force were at different stages of fielding, many of them in the embryonic stage or limited in the resources devoted to logistics units. In some cases, major Army commands took it upon themselves to jump-start the evolution, pursuing the development of systems to satisfy their needs and pursuing the purchase of ITV technologies.

USAREUR had been particularly aggressive in the development and fielding of situational awareness and ITV tools. A relatively large number of 3rd COSCOM's trucks had either movement tracking system (MTS) hardware, the official ITV technology, or defense transportation reporting and control system (DTRACS) hardware, in comparison to the rest of the Army. Thus a good many convoys, even early in OIF, did have one or more trucks with ITV capability. But ITV was often limited to

Figure 6.1
Key Command and Control Characteristics in the Joint Supply Chain Vision
(see pages 13–14)

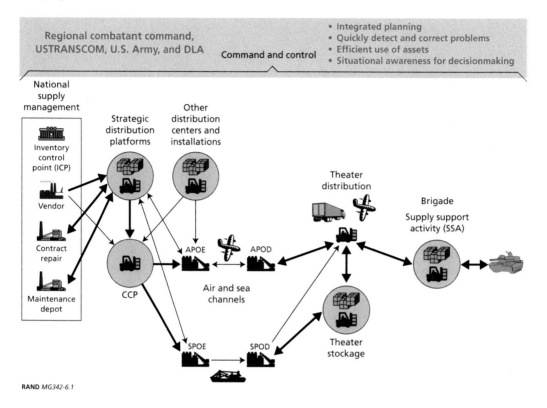

RAND *MG342-6.1*

the trucks and manually entered descriptions of cargo, with few having good radio frequency identification (RFID) data early in operations. From a situational awareness standpoint, a user must have the appropriate automation to see these convoys and what they are carrying. A USAREUR-developed system, the Joint Deployment Logistics Model (JDLM), offered that possibility. However, while the commanding general of the 3rd COSCOM had it on his vehicle and it was installed at CFLCC C-4 in Kuwait, most of the operational units did not have JDLM during combat operations. Additionally, various organizations, such as divisions, had their own self-reported daily supply status reports submitted via spreadsheet. Early communications connectivity problems sometimes hampered the flow of this information, and it could not seamlessly be integrated and provided to all appropriate decisionmakers across the chain of command. The result was limited logistics situational awareness on the battlefield, especially in maneuver units. Brigades often had no visibility of what was in the pipeline to them, to include materiel in the division support area, at DS LSAs, or en route from the TDC. This added to the uncertainty when trying to make tactical and operational decisions, from company to corps level, affecting commanders of all types of units. Further, it made it difficult to determine whether incoming orders were adequate to support their needs, which probably led to some increase in the volume of orders.

Logistics leaders also sometimes lacked situational awareness of friendly forces. Generally, the highly praised Blue Force Tracker was not available to logisticians, up to the commanding general of the COSCOM supporting and maneuvering with V Corps. This forced the COSCOM commanding general to often stay within line-of-sight radio range of forward maneuver units in order to stay abreast of the situation and provide the best possible support.

Difficulties with the command and control of distribution assets have also been attributed to insufficient ITV. If a forward unit "borrowed" trucks, this might not be clear to the COSCOM or TSC. However, we have been unable to document how often such events occurred, with interviews differing in their description of the severity of this problem.

The Monitoring and Control of Processes

Deficiencies in process monitoring and control capabilities led to some supply and distribution problems lingering for significant periods of time. Effective process monitoring and control requires good process management metrics, exception reporting, monitoring systems, and control systems.

Since the mid-1990s, the Army with DLA (through what was formally termed the Velocity Management initiative) and DLA and USTRANSCOM with the services (through what had been known as the Strategic Distribution program) worked to continuously improve processes through a rigorous, Six-Sigma like approach involving process definition and mapping, measurement of performance, and iterative improvement cycles.[1] A series of metrics were instituted to focus on long-term process improvement.

What had received less treatment prior to OIF was the use of metrics for daily or contingency process management and the development of separate metrics focused on such concerns. Leading and quick-feedback metrics and mechanisms were lacking, with reports often provided only on a monthly basis and using a backward-looking technique of just including closed records. This served well for continuous improvement over the long term in a relatively stable environment, even for support of small-scale contingencies, but not for the very dynamic operations of OIF. Additionally, the need for certain metrics had never become apparent—success was assumed in certain areas. The most glaring example of this was the lack of metrics de-

---

[1] John Dumond et al., *Velocity Management: The Business Paradigm That Has Transformed U.S. Army Logistics*, Santa Monica, CA: RAND Corporation, MR-1108-A, 2001.

scribing the success of packing multipacks and building pallets in accordance with theater needs along with associated daily or even hourly exception reports indicating when a SSA's materiel was not being appropriately consolidated in the CCP or the APOEs. Other gaps include the lack of a receipt rate metric, the tracking of whether air versus surface modes of distribution were being used appropriately, shipping cost information, and volume projections or leading indicators.

Over time, many but not all of these gaps in metrics have been addressed through the development of new metrics and reports. We observe much broader and vigilant attention to metrics by the Army and its supply chain partners as OIF has progressed. However, some problems continue to develop without being caught by automation and thus sometimes linger until the right person puts a finger on the problem and gets the attention of the right person in the right organization to fix it. A recent example is that from 21 April to 20 May 2004, most 1st AD shipments went to the 1st Cavalry Division. Once the right people were aware of the problem, it was corrected in a couple of days. Good multipack and pallet purity metrics and exception reports could have caught this within a day, enabling immediate correction. This example also points out that the process complexities and issues that led to early multipack problems still exist. The current transition processes, whether for deployment or redeployment, can fail at many points.

Recommendations

- Continue the implementation of leading indicator and quick-feedback metrics and associated exception reports. Make them broadly available across the supply chain so that not only the owning organization sees performance, but providers and customers of each process do as well. This will let providers understand how they might be affecting downstream flows and gives customers early warning of problems. As necessary, joint solutions can then be developed. We provide recommended metrics aligned with the supply chain vision described in Chapter One. Many are either being prototyped, used internally by the segment process owner, or at a high level in the Army for supply chain oversight.
  - Parts must be available immediately: good ASLs.
    - Fill rate, accommodation rate, satisfaction rate (both fill rate and accommodation rate should be modified to be measured against the population of requests for items that should be stocked in ASLs as described in Chapter Two).
    - Communications status / order flow (daily).
  - For ASLs to be effective, mobile, and affordable: fast, reliable replenishment.
    - Configured loads:

- Pure multipack percentage, Pure pallet percentage, with exception reporting identifying which SSAs are not receiving pure multipacks or pallets and which unit DODAACs are being shipped to the wrong SSAs (daily).

- Frequency channels, adequate capacity, and synchronized flows:
  - Distribution process segment times (air, surface, lateral) – (weekly open records).
  - SDP and CCP volume versus estimated capacity.
  - Node queue times / backlog (daily).

- Stock positioned at originating point of channels:
  - Facing fill at SDPs (percentage of shipments originating at the primary SDP for a geographic region).
  - Theater facing fill in terms of cube and weight.

- For stock to be well positioned: adequate national inventory:
  - Backorder rate (trailing indicator).
  - Queue of orders waiting for OA to be released (leading indicator).

- ITV is essential for these measurements and effective diagnosis of problems:
  - Percentage of shipments with RFID.
  - Percentage of shipments with RFID with level 6 detail (complete addressee and contents data).

- Develop automated process control signaling. Systems that provide metrics should be programmed to signal out-of-control processes and shifts in performance.

- Designate a central organization to identify problems and coordinate rapid response. The designation of USTRANSCOM as the distribution process owner (DPO) satisfies this need. However, the processes by which it will identify problems and coordinate rapid response need to continue to be developed. The newly implemented CENTCOM Deployment/Distribution Operations Center is a move in this direction, but it does not yet have the requisite metrics and information system capabilities to identify the full breadth of potential problems. It and other improvements since the start of OIF do, however, appear to be leading to more rapid, coordinated response and problem resolution once issues are identified. There is now a central point to highlight and bring problems to, which can help when a customer does not know the right person to go to for problem resolution.

- Continue to develop BCS3. This appears to reflect the Army's funded plan, and the Army considers this programmatically on track.[2]

- Develop a plan for ITV of all convoys. This is the Army's intent, and the Army is working to develop an affordable solution to this problem based around the fielding of MTS.[3] The end goal should be to establish positive control over all shipments from origination to destination, so that "losses" can be quickly identified and customers automatically notified.

- Give logistics commanders and staffs adequate operational situational awareness through adequate resourcing of Force XXI Battle Command, Brigade and Below System Blue Force Tracking capability.

---

[2] Briefing, "Connect the Logistician," HQDA-DALO-SMI, 11 May 2004. Army RDT&E Budget Justification (R2 Exhibit), Combat Service Support Control System (Project 091), February 2004.

[3] Briefing, "Connect the Logistician," HQDA-DALO-SMI, 11 May 2004.

CHAPTER SEVEN

Implications for the Future

Toward the Future Force

In some respects, OIF's major combat operations reflected future force operating concepts. Movement was rapid. To a degree, operations were distributed with long, initially unsecured, lines of communication. Logistics was distribution-based. That is, major stockpiles were not built up in the theater or at the DS level; rather, small buffers to provide a little safety margin were employed. The first few days of major combat were conducted as per the pulse vision: no resupply. The remainder of combat operations, not by design, reflected a long spare parts "pulse." Are there implications or lessons for the future force to be found in OIF sustainment, or were the problems simply unique to OIF and current processes and technologies?

Requirements of Distributed Operations with Long LOCs

Once the nature of the enemy was understood, providing rear area and LOC security consumed as many forces as the advance to Baghdad in the V Corps sector. However, it should be noted that different types of forces could be used to do the job than could be used to conduct offensive operations and take Baghdad. Relatively light, mobile forces were determined to be ideal for the mission, with immobile light infantry employed as an expedient, capable backup. Similar issues have recently been identified in Army future force war games. Resulting questions include:

- What are the minimum requirements for logistics units, in particular transportation units, in terms of communications equipment, combat training, weapons, equipment survivability, and personnel, i.e., what is the force protection and internal convoy security need?
- Under what conditions can distributed forces be supported with unsecured LOCs? How does this vary with changes in the capabilities of logistics units?
- What are the logistics unit force protection and LOC security requirements across a range of potential threat, friendly, and environmental conditions?

- What are the right types of forces for LOC security missions, and how, if at all, should this affect the composition of the mix of different future force unit types?

It should be noted that during major combat operations, other than a small number of missions to deliver ammunition and other emergency supplies, little use was made of aviation assets to deliver supplies. This continued until late in 2004. Our research did not delve into the reasons for the dearth of C-130s and other aircraft to support Army forces. The factors that led to this situation should be researched to determine if this was a planning, inter-service coordination, a resource constraint issue, or even a combination of all of these factors.

Low Supply Levels in Maneuver Brigades Produced a Strong Sense of Risk

Maneuver brigades in OIF were often down to one or two days of supplies of food and water and did not always have as much ammunition as they would have liked. Of note, units reached this level despite taking three to four more days of supply than they were expected to consume before the first planned replenishment. Critically, these extra supplies did enable them to make it through disruptions to the supply chain such as the ones caused by the *shamal* and the unexpectedly poor road conditions. Future force operational concepts envision "pulsed" combat operations in which units of action have enough supplies to get through a pulse and are then replenished. By definition, this will result in low supply levels toward the end of pulses. However, one big difference is expected: much better logistics situational awareness. When looking at OIF through the lens of future force operational concepts, several questions come to the fore:

- How would the calculation of risk have changed had the maneuver brigades and the entire chain of command had a good picture of the sustainment flow and the rest of the supply chain?
- How would the level of risk have been viewed had actual conditions been in line with expectations?
- Are the logistics implications of future force operational concepts—operating on the supply edge by the end of combat pulses—in line with soldier expectations?
  - If not, can training bring expectations into alignment?
- What length and types of disruptions should be protected against?
  - What is an acceptable level of supply risk, measured in terms of potential disruptions?
  - How many days of supply should a unit of action carry when it plans to conduct 3-day high-intensity pulses or X-day pulses?

Units Employed a Combat Readiness Standard

During major combat operations, the readiness standard became "shoot-move-communicate" or: "Could a weapon system fire one of its weapons, could it move, and could the soldiers communicate as needed?" The parts needed to correct these types of faults and keep a platform in the action were the only ones crews and mechanics absolutely wanted during combat operations. Everything else could wait until an appropriate break in offensive operations, at which time they would conduct deferred maintenance. However, the shoot-move-communicate standard is an unofficial, undefined standard.

- To what degree does the system-abort standard used in the current requirements and acquisition processes reflect the shoot-move-communicate standard? Should it?
  - What difference might this make in terms of unit spare part requirements?

The Breadth of Equipment in Current BCTs Makes Effective Support Challenging

Current Army brigade combat teams have an incredibly wide breadth of equipment, many of which have low quantities in a brigade. The new modular brigade combat teams have about 30 different major families of equipment requiring substantial numbers of parts. This leads to two problems. First, stocking all of the parts necessary to maintain high readiness for every system requires a very large SSA, or the readiness of some systems has to be sacrificed. Second, the demand rate for most of the parts for the systems with low quantities is too low for reasonably efficient stockage within the SSA, as most parts are needed once or less per year, making support of these systems more difficult. Thus, the drive to increased commonality for future forces has the potential to both increase support effectiveness and reduce inventory needs and the associated unit size. The current Future Combat Systems (FCS) unit of action design will reduce the number of unique families to be supported by about 7, each of which are among the more complex systems requiring large breadths of parts. While commonality should not be pursued to too great a detriment in terms of capabilities, backing away from commonality should only be done after consideration of the support effects.

Improving the Logistics System for Current and Future Forces

The chapters of this report have been organized around the major processes of the proposed joint supply chain vision, including command and control: the nervous system and "brain" that monitor how the body is working and make the muscles move together to take action. Within each, specific problems and their causes were identified. However, common themes and lessons span across many of them in different portions of the supply chain.

The supply chain needs to be integrated with a common supply chain vision.

Many of the OIF sustainment problems identified in this report were the result of elements of the supply chain not being aligned with other parts of the system or designed without a clear, focused purpose within the broader supply chain. Underlying this appears to be the lack of a common supply chain vision that lays out the complementary roles of the various supply levels and the connecting distribution channels. A common vision is needed to ensure that each process and organization is aligned with a common goal. From an overall supply chain vision, the purpose of each element within the chain can then be defined in order to focus its mission. A decision to use theater supply, for example, to reduce airlift consumption for sustainment has implications for theater supply doctrine and organizational design, AWRS stocks, strategic transportation, CONUS distribution centers, and national supply. Each of these must be done "right" to achieve this aim. Similarly, how the Army designs its units and theater distribution system capabilities, and how loads are built and delivered to the theater must be aligned for smooth distribution flow.

- The Army should work with its supply chain partners through efforts led by the distribution process owner to develop a common vision of an integrated supply chain. The complementary, not redundant, roles of each inventory location (not necessarily echelon), distribution node, and distribution channel should be defined.
  - Review doctrine, organizational designs, training, equipment, information systems, facilities, policies, and practices for alignment with the supply chain vision and defined roles within the supply chain. This is a check of internal consistency.
    - The review needs to include how well processes, resources, and capacities are prepared to enable rapid, effective transitions for contingency operations, which affect unit locations and demand levels. For example, coordinating changes in load consolidation requirements was unwieldy in OIF, leading to delays and mistakes. Tactical ASLs did not have the capacity to handle wartime conditions and were not effectively adjusted. In terms of national providers, only strategic transportation capacity was able to seamlessly contract and expand to demands. It has the unique opportunity to bring on flexible contracted capacity in steps of one aircraft or ship, to include the trained crew. This contrasts with warehouse and distribution center capacity and especially with national spare parts requirements.

— Ensure that each element of the supply chain is mutually supporting, producing external consistency. The assumptions embedded within the design of each element of the supply chain with regard to other parts of the supply chain should be checked to ensure that they reflect realistic capabilities.

— Improve the joint understanding of the unique field requirements of the services. Ensure that joint organizations understand each service's information systems, unit capabilities, and processes. Likewise, the services need to understand DLA, USTRANSCOM, and General Services Agency (GSA) processes and information requirements, as well as those of private-sector providers.

• Metrics should be adopted to maintain alignment with the vision, with command and control aided by automated signaling systems for process monitoring and control.

Information system resourcing for logistics units needs higher priority.

This is not new to OIF, but new operational and logistics concepts are making this ever more important. Non-line-of-sight, mobile communications are clearly essential for logistics forces, as are the situational awareness tools needed to conduct distribution over extended distances, often over less than completely secured LOCs. To operate effectively with lean sustainment forces, it is imperative that logisticians be able to respond quickly to changes in the battlefield situation, which demands a high level of friendly situational awareness. Good logistics data transformed into situational awareness is crucial to support of distributed operations, effective and efficient use of logistics assets, operational planning, and process monitoring and control.

Stability operations can be logistically demanding in their own right and need adequate treatment in planning.

While there were certainly sustainment problems associated with major combat operations, others were specifically driven by the long-continuing high demands of stability and support operations and the conduct of counterinsurgency operations. In particular, national-level providers were not prepared for long-term operations; this is not surprising, as such operations are not generally embedded in the formal contingency planning process used to determine logistics resource requirements. This includes the Army's force structure and AWRS stocks planning.

Deliberate planning guidance should be reviewed to assess whether the scenarios provide an adequate basis for resource planning. Planning for contingency operations should include consideration of stability operation requirements: what does it take to "win the peace"? Within the Army, this would affect the force structure process and AWRS stock determination. Sustaining high levels of support may also have implications for how DLA and USTRANSCOM design strategic distribution capacity.

Similarly, potential stability operations scenarios should be considered during crisis action planning to identify resource requirements.

Resourcing processes should consider uncertainty and the implications of capacity shortages.

Developing a backlog or otherwise falling short of logistics capacity early in an operation is particularly problematic because it is extremely difficult to recover from, resulting in an extended period of poor support. Once a backlog develops, capacity must not only ramp up to meet the higher, ongoing level of contingency demand; it must also include extra, temporary capacity beyond that needed to handle incoming demand to work off the backlog. This has two implications. First, supply and force risk assessments during planning should recognize the long-term operational effects of insufficient capacity, affecting decisions about how much slack or buffer capacity should be in the system. Second, surprises must be expected. Thus, resourcing processes must be responsive, with decisionmakers made fully cognizant of the implications of delay, and the supply chain from the industrial base to tactical distribution capability must be agile enough to respond. Failures in these areas in OIF led to inadequate intra-theater transportation capacity, leading to high supply risk during major combat operations, inadequate distribution center capacity resulting in slow strategic distribution for a period of nine months, and excessive shortages of spare parts from which a recovery is still not fully complete.

Joint training should be extended to exercise the entire logistics system.

There are many critical actions that have to be executed to support a contingency that involve processes not normally performed in the course of peacetime operations. If these are never practiced, it will be difficult to execute them well when a contingency develops. Moreover, knowledge of the process may be lost altogether. The transition-to-war problems occurred in part because of processes that were insufficient to handle the problem. They also occurred due to insufficient practice. This extends from the tactical level to the national system, beginning with contingency planning. The Army should review all wartime and contingency processes from the tactical to the national level to determine which are not exercised in training with all requisite joint and interagency organizations participating. The same review should determine which tasks do not have adequate doctrine and mission training plans.

At the tactical level, when units go to Combat Training Centers, they should have to set up logistics operations from scratch as they would in a real deployment. For example, if units are to receive new DODAACs for operations, the SSA should have to set up a SARSS computer with a new DODAAC. From a national perspective, this DODAAC needs to flow through Army channels to DLA, which should practice the DODAAC changeover process in its distribution center operations.

Theater support commands need to plan theater distribution systems, theater distribution centers and warehouses need to be set up, and ports need to be opened. AMC and DLA need to exercise contingency planning processes to determine supply requirements for specific operational plans. Even the financial change and approval process should be exercised. Conducting exercises to practice these infrequent events is the only way to ensure that personnel will know how to conduct these contingency-focused activities. The exercises will also reveal process and materiel roadblocks as well as opportunities for improvement.

Planning tools and organizational structures need to better support expeditionary operations.

First, to support fast-paced, frequently changing expeditionary operations, logistics system planners need effective automation to rapidly determine unit requirements. Second, organizational structures should be designed to enable these requirements to be easily and quickly resourced. Building blocks need to be the right size and modular to quickly provide initial capabilities and then seamless ramp-up capacity as the total force builds. Third, the structures and automation should support effective deployment planning. That is, the requirements justification should be clear. This depends upon two things: good analytic support for capacity requirements and well-defined linkages between unit types and capabilities.

A Logistics System that Has Transformed in Concept but Is Still in Transition

It should be recognized that logistically there was a fundamental shift between Operation Desert Storm (ODS) in 1991 and OIF in 2003. From an intent standpoint, OIF marked a de facto application of what has become known as distribution based logistics (DBL). DBL means limited inventory to cover small disruptions in distribution flow and enough supply to cover consumption between replenishments, with the primary reliance on frequent, reliable distribution rather than on large forward stockpiles.[1] This is roughly how OIF combat operations were conducted. Except for small buffer stocks, such as one or two days of food and water at logistics support areas, supplies stayed at what could be considered an intermediate support base (ISB) (i.e., Kuwait) and were not pushed forward in large amounts.[2] Although healthier,

---

[1] Note that "small" and "large" are simply relative terms. There is no definitive threshold in terms of forward inventory size between a DBL and a non-DBL system. Rather, there is a continuum of possibilities.

[2] While Kuwait is considered "in theater," it has been outside the hostile "combat" zone of operations. Depending upon the theater and contingency, the types of operations in Kuwait might be done outside of the theater. The decision will likely come down to distances and threat conditions.

even forward fuel supplies were limited to a few days. Further, the supply levels at the ISB in Kuwait remained limited—days of supplies instead of weeks, as at the forward logistics bases near the Iraqi border for ODS.

However, many of the enablers of DBL were immature, such as in-transit visibility of supplies, or not fielded, such as mobile, non-line-of-sight logistics communications capabilities. Nor were many of the processes fully aligned with DBL concepts, reflecting a lack of supply chain integration and of a common vision of a DBL supply chain. In short, many of the critical elements of a DBL system were not in place, leading to shortfalls in performance that were overcome in OIF but that also increased risk.

The experience points to numerous issues, but several observations should be highlighted. Operating in this way may not always be comfortable for commanders and the troops, especially if this is not what they are used to. This is particularly true without complete, accurate, and real-time information on current and projected supply levels, the absence of which raises the perceived level of risk when relying on distribution. And with limited forward and ISB supplies, problems can develop quickly. Thus, to counter potential risk, commanders need to quickly know about and resolve any distribution flow and supply issues, demanding effective process monitoring and control. Additionally, to reduce uncertainty and to support operational decision-making, DBL demands solid logistics situational awareness.

With a supply point model of support, portions of the supply chain can be somewhat disconnected for periods of time. In DBL, planning and execution must be integrated across the entire system from CONUS to consuming units, requiring adequate lift capacity balanced across distribution segments, seamless transfer of loads at distribution nodes, and load configurations aligned with distribution node capabilities. Without large stockpiles of items with high demand variability, such as spare parts, units need to be always connected physically and electronically to order and "pull" such items when they use the few they have. Such items cannot be effectively "pushed" like items with low demand variability, such as food, which are used at relatively predictable rates.

Lastly, the desired levels of acceptable risk and associated buffers in a DBL system need to be carefully examined. The severe sandstorm a few days into OIF ground combat generated an example of how a two- to three-day disruption can affect a force that is operating with limited supplies. The system was able to handle this, but just barely.

Along these lines, the common thread in most post-OIF reports and plans is not to abandon DBL but to determine how to make it work, particularly in expeditionary operations.

Outline of Recommendations

1. Tactical Supply

1.1. Ensure that SSA warehouse capacities are sufficient to meet readiness needs.

1.2. APS ASLs:

   1.2.1. Improve the methodology used to determine APS ASL requirements.

   1.2.2. Compute ROs and ROPs.

   1.2.3. Evaluate the effectiveness of the review and oversight process.

   1.2.4. The Army should establish APS ASLs as turnkey operations.

   1.2.5. Ensure that all APS ASLs are used on a periodic basis in exercises.

1.3. Home station (deployable) ASLs:

   1.3.1. Embed recent improvements made to the current methodology (termed enhanced dollar cost banding) in automation.

   1.3.2. Stock to wartime depth within storage constraints.

   1.3.3. Centralize requirements determination, with unit review and approval.

      1.3.3.1. Develop automation to support rapid ASL computation for task organizations.

      1.3.3.2. In the interim or as a first step, use the recently stood up Army Materiel Command centralized ASL expert team to produce customized ASLs.

1.4. The Army should analyze inventory options for dynamic battlefield task organization.

1.5. Better align ASL performance metrics to focus only on parts desired for stockage.

1.6. Communications connectivity:

1.6.1. Improve ability to create requests, especially during combat operations.

1.6.2. Enable always-on, mobile requisition submission capability.

2. Theater Distribution

2.1. Develop improved, integrated theater distribution planning automation.

2.2. Develop integrated, modular theater sustainment capabilities.

2.2.1. Develop a clear mapping of unit types to capabilities to mission needs.

2.2.2. Ensure that unit building blocks are the right size.

2.3. At a minimum, plan and, to the extent possible, set up distribution systems in exercises from brigade to theater level.

2.4. Align water supply and distribution policies/planning and execution.

2.5. DoD should designate a theater distribution system integrator or owner within a regional combatant command.

3. Strategic Distribution

3.1. Work with USTRANSCOM as the distribution process owner (DPO) and DLA to ensure that single or SSA-pure multipacks and pallets are in joint policy.

3.2. With DLA, the Army should work to develop mechanisms to ensure that DODAAC and sortation logic remains up to date.

3.2.1. The Army and DLA should develop a standardized process for communicating DODAAC and support relationship changes.

3.2.2. DLA should improve its internal process for entering DODAAC and support relationship changes in DSS.

3.2.3. The Army should develop a standard deployment DODAAC policy.

3.3. As a customer, the Army should work with DLA to assess whether it has sufficiently rapid and adequate distribution center and CCP capacity expansion capabilities, and should assist DLA in developing improved strategies for meeting contingency capacity requirements.

3.4. Examine CCP bypass policy and coding: what role should aerial ports play?

3.5.   Develop long-term aerial port pallet-build policies.

4. National- and Theater-Level Supply

4.1.   Develop doctrine and associated policy for theater stockage that limit inventory requirements for forward positioned items to those items that drive readiness or consume substantial airlift, and that are cost-effective to stock forward at surface replenishment depth.

   4.1.1.   Integrate with APS forward positioned WRSI policy and requirements determination.

   4.1.2.   Limit APS insurance items to CONUS-based war reserve.

   4.1.3.   Generally set inventory levels to support surface replenishment.

      4.1.3.1.   Reduce surface replenishment times.

   4.1.4.   Consider including small or expensive readiness drivers in forward stockage with the depth requirement based upon air replenishment in only those cases in which theater lateral time is substantially faster than strategic distribution.

4.2.   Improve the APS requirements determination methodology.

4.3.   Make the APS WRSI into turnkey GS SSAs.

4.4.   Develop a standard, accurate, and fast process for changing requirements and allocating obligation authority for national inventory increases and a production surge, as needed, to support contingencies as they develop.

   4.4.1.   Redesign the contingency requirements determination process.

   4.4.2.   Apply risk management techniques for contingency budget approval.

   4.4.3.   Review the obligation authority change and release process to identify opportunities for improving process speed.

4.5.   Conduct AMC and HQDA exercises to produce and review contingency requirements and to execute the financial approval process.

4.6.   Continue and accelerate efforts to reduce administrative, production, and repair lead times in order to reduce AMC's replenishment lead times.

5. Command and Control

5.1.   Continue the implementation of leading indicator and quick-feedback metrics and associated exception reports.

5.2.   Develop automated process control signaling.

5.3.   Designate a central organization to identify problems and coordinate rapid response.

5.4.   Continue to develop the Battle Command Sustainment Support System (BCS3).

5.5.   Develop a plan for ITV of all convoys.

5.6.   Give logistics commanders and staffs adequate operational situational awareness through adequate resourcing of Force XXI Battle Command, Brigade and Below System Blue Force Tracking capability.

6.   Overarching Recommendations

6.1.   Supply chain planning needs to be better integrated with a common supply chain vision.

    6.1.1.   The newly designated distribution process owner (USTRANS-COM), in concert with the Army, the other services, and DLA, should develop and promulgate a common vision of an integrated supply chain. The complementary, not redundant roles, of each inventory location, distribution node, and distribution channel should be defined.

    6.1.2.   Every joint logistics organization should examine and refine its processes to ensure detailed alignment with this vision. Review doctrine, organizational designs, training, equipment, information systems, facilities, policies, and practices for alignment with the supply chain vision and defined roles within the supply chain.

    6.1.3.   The assumptions embedded within the design of each element of the supply chain with regard to other parts of the supply chain should be checked to ensure that they reflect realistic capabilities.

    6.1.4.   Improve the joint understanding of the unique field requirements of the services. Likewise, the services need to understand DLA, USTRANSCOM, and GSA processes and information requirements, as well as those of private-sector providers.

    6.1.5.   Metrics should be adopted to maintain alignment with the vision.

6.2.   Logistics information systems need adequate levels of resources to provide non-line-of-sight mobile communications and effective logistics situational awareness in order to make new and emerging operational and logistics concepts feasible.

6.3. Deliberate and contingency planning should include improved consideration of the logistics resource requirements necessary to execute sustained stability and support operations.

6.4. Resourcing processes should consider uncertainty and implications of capacity shortages.

   6.4.1. The flexibility of financial and resource allocation processes to rapidly respond to the need for dramatic changes in logistics capacity that sometimes arises from operational forecast error should be improved.

   6.4.2. Logistics resource decisions should more explicitly consider how much buffer capacity should be provided in order to handle typical operational and demand variability without the development of large backlogs.

6.5. Joint training should be extended to exercise the entire logistics system.

   6.5.1. The Army should review all wartime and contingency processes from the tactical to the national level to determine which are not exercised in training with all requisite joint organizations participating. Such processes range from setting up tactical logistics information systems to planning a theater distribution architecture to determining national level spare parts distribution center capacity requirements.

   6.5.2. Review which tasks and processes do not have adequate doctrine and mission training plans.

6.6. Planning tools and organizational structures need to better support expeditionary operations.

   6.6.1. Automation should more effectively support the identification of logistics unit requirements to support a given operation.

   6.6.2. Unit "building blocks" should be the right size and modular to quickly and effectively provide initial theater capabilities and then to facilitate the seamless ramp-up of capacity and capability as a deployment matures.

Key Terms

Distribution: The process of moving materiel from a source to final destination, including the use and management of transportation resources, packaging, transshipment and cross-docking operations.

Movement control: The command and control of transportation assets to ensure that they are effectively used to meet distribution needs.

Supply: The acquisition and receipt, storage, issue, and management of materiel.

Supply chain management: The process of orchestrating all of the functions and processes that combine to provide needed materiel to consumers.

Sustainment: The provision of personnel, logistical, and other support required to maintain and prolong operations or combat until successful accomplishment or revision of the mission or of the national objective.

Transportation: The function and assets used to move materiel and personnel.

References

2/3 ID: interviews with CPT Jeff Sabatini (A/S-4 Maint and S&S), 1LT Adam Points (Battle Captain), and focus group on 29 October 2003.

3rd ID Division Artillery (DIVARTY): interviews with LTC Craig Finley (CDR 1/39 FA BN MLRS), MAJ Phil Rice (Ops, 1/9), MAJ Jim Rooker (Asst S-3), MAJ Benigno (S-3, 1/39), SGT Pichardo, CPT Miguel Garcia (S-4), MAJ Barren (2 BDE Fire Support Officer), MAJ Ken Patterson (current XO), COL Thomas Torrance (CDR) on 28 October 2003.

3-7 CAV: interviews with CPT Patrick Shea, 1LT Keith Miller, CPT David Muhlenkamp on 29 October 2003.

Army RDT&E Budget Justification (R2 Exhibit), Combat Service Support Control System (Project 091), February 2004.

Army Materiel Command, *Theater Logistics in the Gulf War*, 1994.

Baca, MAJ Glenn, formerly Division Transportation Officer (XO 703 MSB), interview with the author, 28 October 2003.

Blount, MG Buford C., Commanding General, 3rd Infantry Division (Mechanized), interview with the author, 18 November 2003.

Conway, LtGen James, commander, First Marine Expeditionary Force, "Live Briefing from Iraq," 30 May 2003, http://www.defenselink.mil/transcripts/2003/tr20030530-0229.html.

Cook, LTC Katherine, email discussion with Eric Peltz, 2 June 2004.

Cook, LTC Katherine, email to Eric Peltz, 20 June 2004.

Deputy Chief of Staff, G-4, Headquarters, Department of the Army, "Connect Army Logisticians," Army Logistics White Paper, October 2004.

Deputy Chief of Staff, G-4, Headquarters, Department of the Army, "Delivering Materiel Readiness to the Army," Army Logistics White Paper, December 2003.

Deputy Chief of Staff, G-4, Headquarters, Department of the Army, "Improve Force Reception," Army Logistics White Paper, October 2004.

Deputy Chief of Staff, G-4, Headquarters, Department of the Army, "Integrate the Supply Chain," Army Logistics White Paper, October 2004.

Deputy Chief of Staff, G-4, Headquarters, Department of the Army, "Modernize Theater Distribution," Army Logistics White Paper, October 2004.

Dumond, John, et al., *Velocity Management: The Business Paradigm That Has Transformed U.S. Army Logistics,* Santa Monica, CA: RAND Corporation, MR-1108-A, 2001.

Fletcher, BG Charles, former commanding general of 3rd COSCOM, interview with Eric Peltz and David Oaks, 22 October 2003.

Fontenot, COL (ret.) Gregory, LTC E. J. Degen, and LTC David Tohn, *On Point: The United States Army in Operation Iraqi Freedom,* Fort Leavenworth, KS: Combat Studies Institute Press, 2004.

Girardini, Kenneth, Eric Peltz, Thomas Held, Art Lackey, and Candice Riley, *Army Logistics in Operation Iraqi Freedom: Spare Parts Demand Analysis and ASL Performance*, unpublished research, January 2004.

Girardini, Kenneth, and Eric Peltz, *Sustainment of Army Forces in Operation Iraqi Freedom: Prepositioned Authorized Stockage Lists*, unpublished research, August 2004.

Girardini, Kenneth, Eric Peltz, Art Lackey, Elvira Loredo, and Candice Riley, *Sustainment of Army Forces in Operation Iraqi Freedom: Army War Reserve Sustainment Stocks*, unpublished research, August 2004.

Girardini, Kenneth, Arthur Lackey, Kristin Leuschner, Dan Relles, Mark Totten, and Darlene Blake, *Dollar Cost Banding: A New Algorithm for Computing Inventory Levels for Army SSAs*, Santa Monica, CA: RAND Corporation, MG-128-A, 2004.

Kleppinger, COL Tim, "LCOP Logistics Common Operating Picture Key to BCS3," briefing, February 2004.

Landis, Jeff, U.S. Army Materiel Systems Analysis Activity, "War Reserve and Iraqi Freedom Demands," 5 November 2003, briefing.

Lee, COL James, Support Operations Officer, 377th Theater Support Command, email to Eric Peltz, 20 July 2004.

Lee, COL James, Support Operations Officer, 377th Theater Support Command, interview with Eric Peltz, John Halliday, and John Bondanella.

Lyons, LTC Steve, formerly commander of 703rd Main Support Battalion, 3rd Infantry Division, (Division Deputy Chief of Staff, G-4), interview with Eric Peltz and Marc Robbins, 28 October 2003.

McKiernan, LTG David, "U.S. Department of Defense Briefing on Operation Iraqi Freedom," briefing, 23 April 2003: www.defenselink.mil/transcripts/2003/tr20030423-0122.html.

Motsek, Gary, Deputy DCS, G-3, AMC, interview with Eric Peltz.

Mullen, William, Office of the DCS, G-3, AMC, interview with Eric Peltz.

Murphree, MAJ Thomas, TDC Commander (and previously CFLCC C-4 Battle Captain), interview with Eric Peltz, 26 May 2004.

Office of the DCS, G-3, AMC, "030603 inventory update v3," briefing.

Office of the DCS, G-3, AMC, "030611 budget audit trail v4," spreadsheet.

Office of the DCS, G-3, AMC, "FY03 AMC AWCF Releases Close-v3.0," spreadsheet.

"Operational Requirements Document for the Battle Command Sustainment Support System (BCS3) (Combat Service Support Control System (CSSCS))," Change Number 3.7, 5 November 2003.

Pacheco, MAJ Ron, 3rd COSCOM S-3 shop (now ERD), interview with Eric Peltz, September 2003.

Peltz, Eric, Marc L. Robbins, Patricia Boren, and Melvin Wolff, *Diagnosing the Army's Equipment Readiness: The Equipment Downtime Analyzer*, Santa Monica, CA: RAND Corporation, MR-1481-A, 2002.

Peltz, Eric, John Halliday, Marc Robbins, and Ken Girardini, *Sustainment of Army Forces in Operation Iraqi Freedom: Battlefield Logistics and Effects on Operations*, unpublished research, August 2004.

Peltz, Eric, and Jeffrey Angers, *Sustainment of Army Forces in Operation Iraqi Freedom: Determining and Resourcing Spare Part Requirements*, unpublished research.

Robbins, Marc, and Eric Peltz, *Sustainment of Army Forces in Operation Iraqi Freedom: End to End Distribution*, unpublished research, August 2004.

Robbins, Marc L., Patricia Boren, and Kristin Leuschner, *The Strategic Distribution System in Support of Operation Enduring Freedom*, Santa Monica, CA: RAND Corporation, DB-428-USTC/DLA, 2004 (http://www.rand.org/publications/DB/DB428/).

Rogers, COL James, Commander, Division Support Command, 101st Airborne Division (Air Assault), interview with Eric Peltz and Marc Robbins, August 2003.

V Corps, Department of the Army, "The Road to 'Victory!' in Operation Iraqi Freedom," briefing.

Wallace, LTG William, former commanding general of V Corps, interview with Eric Peltz and LTC Chris McCurry (CASCOM), Fort Leavenworth, KS, 6 April 2004.

Wang, Mark Y. D., *Accelerated Logistics: Streamlining the Army's Supply Chain*, Santa Monica, CA: RAND Corporation, MR-1140-A, 2000.

Williams, LTC Willie, formerly Commander, 26th FSB, 3rd Infantry Division, interview with Eric Peltz and David Oaks, 22 October 2003.